The Case for a
Job Guarantee

"More than any other piece of public policy, the Job Guarantee can help us build a more equitable economy and just society. Pavlina Tcherneva has written the perfect primer for anyone interested in understanding why and how the Job Guarantee can do so much good."

Ady Barkan, activist, organizer and author of *Eyes to the Wind*

"Many are coming to understand that the socioeconomic system in which we live – or endure – is broken, badly. There are solutions. The ideas in this valuable work point the way to a more civilized, indeed survivable, social order."

Noam Chomsky

"The Job Guarantee is the next big, common-sense idea for economic reform. Over years of dedicated work, Pavlina Tcherneva has developed and advanced the plan, and today it stands poised to complement the Green New Deal and Medicare for All as a fundamental pillar of the progressive agenda. Read about it here … and go out to help make it happen."

James K. Galbraith, The University of Texas at Austin

"Tcherneva lays out the case for how we can raise the roof by lifting the floor, as we transition away from a failed and cruel economy based on an assumed percentage of unemployment. She demonstrates how a jobs guarantee can help address some of our biggest challenges, including bridging the gap to a Green New Deal and the critical conversion from a fossil-fuel economy to a sustainable future. Through her book we can see a world where everyone who wants to claim the dignity of work as their own has that right."

Sara Nelson, International President, Association of Flight Attendants-CWA, AFL-CIO

"Pavlina Tcherneva offers an eloquent and convincing argument for a public sector job guarantee as an economic shock absorber. Particularly valuable is her demonstration of how such a program can revitalise local communities. Beyond this, her book is an indispensable primer for advocates of a Green New Deal."

Lord Robert Skidelsky, author of *Keynes: The Return of the Master*

For my daughter Yvette –
May you live in a world that is green and just.

Pavlina R. Tcherneva

The Case for a Job Guarantee

polity

Copyright © Pavlina R. Tcherneva 2020

The right of Pavlina R. Tcherneva to be identified as Author of this Work has been
asserted in accordance with the UK Copyright, Designs and Patents Act 1988.

First published in 2020 by Polity Press
Reprinted 2020

Polity Press
65 Bridge Street
Cambridge CB2 1UR, UK

Polity Press
101 Station Landing
Suite 300
Medford, MA 02155, USA

ISBN-13: 978-1-5095-4209-3
ISBN-13: 978-1-5095-4210-9 (pb)

A catalogue record for this book is available from the British Library.

Typeset in 11 on 15 Sabon by Servis Filmsetting Ltd, Stockport, Cheshire
Printed and bound in the United States by LSC Communications

The publisher has used its best endeavours to ensure that the URLs for external
websites referred to in this book are correct and active at the time of going to
press. However, the publisher has no responsibility for the websites and can
make no guarantee that a site will remain live or that the content is or will remain
appropriate.

Every effort has been made to trace all copyright holders, but if any have been
overlooked the publisher will be pleased to include any necessary credits in any
subsequent reprint or edition.

For further information on Polity, visit our website: politybooks.com

Contents

Acknowledgments

When I first began working on the Job Guarantee in the late 1990s, the consensus was that the US had reached full employment and the Goldilocks economy was here to stay. The argument made little sense but it convinced me that researching unemployment would be a solitary experience. Happily, I was wrong.

My journey began with the friendship and support of Mathew Forstater, Warren Mosler, and L. Randall Wray, and connected me to collaborators and friends, including William Mitchell, Stephanie Kelton, Fadhel Kaboub, Scott Fullwiler, among many others. The fellowship of the Job Guarantee grew. I met people from the US and abroad who enriched my work. They hailed from all corners of academia – from history and law, to public policy and the humanities. I worked with

Acknowledgments

policy makers who were designing and implementing similar programs. Environmental and social justice activists, youth organizations, journalists, and engaged citizens embraced the proposal. They have all contributed to where we are today, namely a place where the Job Guarantee is once again part of the national conversation and policy agenda.

While writing this book, I benefited greatly from conversations with Angela Glover Blackwell, Raúl Carrillo, Grégor Chapelle, William "Sandy" Darity, Isabelle Ferreras, Trudy Goldberg, Rohan Gray, Darrick Hamilton, Philip Harvey, Sarah Treuhaft, and many others. My thanks to three anonymous referees and my editor George Owers, whose comments greatly improved this volume, and to my student Kirsten Ostbirk who helped with figures and references. Special thanks to John Henry for his generous feedback, often wrapped in some much needed humor. Needless to say, all opinions herein and any remaining errors are my own. Finally, my deepest gratitude goes to my family for their support, and especially to Douglas Johnson, who makes everything possible.

Preface

In the blink of an eye, millions lost their jobs. Like an inferno barreling across the globe, the coronavirus pandemic shutters one economy after another. Labor markets are cratering and the wave of layoffs has already turned into a tsunami. The Federal Reserve forecasts that US unemployment will surpass its 1930s Great Depression levels. And on the heels of this pandemic will come another – the suffering and devastation that result from mass unemployment.

This book was written before the hemorrhage in the labor market began. Yet it enumerates the many ways in which unemployment behaves like a silent epidemic – even while the economy is humming near full employment – from the way it spreads, to its virulent nature, to the enormous social costs it inflicts on people, communities, and the economy. In just a few short months, these costs would be immeasurable.

The pandemic has exposed as farcical many of the conversations from yesterday. Raising the minimum wage to

Preface

$15/hour, we were told, would cost jobs (as if workers in poverty were ever good for the economy). Today, it's obvious that the people on whose labor we vitally depend are the very same people who cannot secure living wages and basic job protections. Store clerks, dispatchers, warehouse workers, delivery drivers, and sanitation staff are now lauded as "essential workers," but when the economy recovers, will the experts once again call them low-productivity employees whose jobs are in need of automation?

Yesterday, most presidential hopefuls shunned the idea that the government could provide universal healthcare. Today, we see not only that it can, but that it absolutely must, as millions lose their health insurance along with their jobs.

Yesterday, economists begrudgingly admitted that, despite historically low unemployment rates, the economy was nowhere near full employment and millions of people still wanted good jobs. Today, we face the daunting task of returning to those low rates after reaching double-digit unemployment. It took more than ten years to do so after the Great Financial Crisis of 2008. How long will it take now?

This book critiques the conventional stabilization approaches that produce prolonged and painful jobless recoveries. And if we have to face another one, would economists insist tomorrow that we have reached a permanently high "natural rate of unemployment?" Will they rekindle the old "structural unemployment" excuses for the abject failure of public policy to do what it can and what is right, namely to employ the unemployed?

We need a Job Guarantee now more than ever. The following pages present the case for its overwhelming benefits and a blueprint for its implementation. Its design is inspired precisely by the way policy is supposed to respond to pandemics, by prioritizing preparedness and prevention. Decades of austerity have led to the erosion of essential public sector programs, services, and institutional capacities, leaving us woefully unprepared to respond to this pandemic and the social crisis that will follow. The public was baited into accepting austerity with the myth that the federal government could run out of funding. And yet, almost overnight, the US government passed an unprecedented $2.2 trillion package to tackle the pandemic, with additional spending on the way according to bipartisan consensus. Many countries around the world are doing the same. Finding the money was never the problem. Finding the political will to rally behind key policies always was.

Tomorrow, when politicians ask "but how will the government pay for this program?," the answer should always be "the way we paid for the pandemic." If we can pay for all the interventions necessary to stem this crisis, we surely can afford to guarantee jobs, homes, healthcare, and a green economy. What we cannot afford is to emerge out of this moment with the same economic problems and inequalities that created so much suffering and devastation even before the current pandemic.

Introduction

It is not because things are difficult that we do not dare, it is because we do not dare that they are difficult.

– Seneca

"There are no guarantees in life" is a familiar refrain, as is "if you really want something, you have to work for it." But what if what you really want is paid work – a decent, well-paid job? And what if you cannot find it because, well, there are no guarantees in life?

This is the paradox the Job Guarantee proposal aims to solve. It is a public policy that provides an employment opportunity on standby to anyone looking for work, no matter their personal circumstances or the state of the economy. It converts the unemployment offices into employment offices to provide voluntary public service work opportunities in a wide range of care, environmental, rehabilitation, and small infrastructure projects. The Job Guarantee is a public option for jobs.

The *guarantee* part of the proposal is the promise, the assurance, that a basic job offer will always be available to those who seek it. The *job* part deals with another paradox, namely that while paid work in the modern world is life-defining and indispensable, it has, for many, become elusive, onerous, and punitive. The job component in the Job Guarantee aims to change all that by establishing a decent, living-wage job as a standard for all jobs in the economy, while paving the way for the transformation of public policy, the nature of the work experience, and the meaning of work itself.

The Job Guarantee deals with two very specific aspects of economic insecurity: unemployment (intermittent or long-term), and poorly paid employment (precarious and unequal). There are other labor market problems such as wage theft, discrimination, poverty, and stagnant income growth. And there are other forms of economic insecurity too, such as the lack of affordable and high quality food, care, housing, and education, or a lack of protection from the ravages of climate change. While, in a certain sense, the Job Guarantee has a narrow and clear mission – to provide a decent job at decent pay to all jobseekers who come a-knocking – by its very nature and design it addresses a wide range of social and economic problems and helps deliver a fairer economy.

At bottom, the Job Guarantee is a policy of care, one that fundamentally rejects the notion that people in economic distress, communities in disrepair, and an environment in peril are the unfortunate but unavoidable collateral damage of a market economy.

The idea of using public policy to guarantee the right to employment is not new. Its long life and resilience stem from its deep moral content. It was affirmed in the Universal Declaration of Human Rights and in President Franklin Delano Roosevelt's proposed Economic Bill of Rights, it was a signature issue in the struggle for civil rights, and it is etched into many nations' constitutions (inspired by the Universal Declaration). But its mandate remains unmet. In the US, the architects of the 1946 Employment Act and the 1978 Full Employment and Balanced Growth Act tried, but ultimately failed, to implement appropriate legislation to secure it. In the absence of a universal right to work, intermittent direct employment programs around the world have attempted, however imperfectly, to fill the void, many with perceptible success.

Introduction

Today, the Job Guarantee has been hailed as "the single most crucial aspect of the Green New Deal,"[1] conveying that environmental justice cannot be delivered without economic and social justice. The Green New Deal and the Job Guarantee aim to resolve two seemingly distinct, but in fact organically inseparable, existential problems – those of climate change and economic insecurity. What good is a green future in which the dangers of global warming have abated, but families and whole communities continue to experience deaths of despair due to poverty, unemployment, and economic distress? And what kind of an economy would it be which made well-paid jobs available to all, but continued to exploit and devastate the natural environment on which we vitally depended?

Although the Job Guarantee predates the Green New Deal, it has always been *green* – from the days of Roosevelt's Tree Army to modern proposals like the one outlined in this book – prioritizing environmental conservation and community renewal. The Green New Deal is an ambitious policy agenda designed to transform the economy and deliver a habitable planet to future generations. The Job Guarantee embeds economic and social justice into the scientific response to climate change; it is an indispensable part of the green agenda that would ensure that no one would be left behind in the transition. But it is also a transformative macroeconomic policy and safety net that would tackle decades-long labor market problems along with the dislocations that would emerge from the greening process. Put simply, the Job Guarantee ensures that, while we work to protect the environment and transform the economy, we have a policy that protects working people and transforms the work experience itself.

This book presents the Job Guarantee proposal and explains why it is critical to the climate movement. It also contends that, even after the Green New Deal has fulfilled its mission, a market economy would still require a Job Guarantee. This is because the program serves as an ongoing shock absorber and a powerful tool for economic stabilization, which is perhaps its most critical macroeconomic feature. It was absent in the era of industrialization, when paid work became the indispensable yet unreliable ticket to securing a livelihood. It was missing in the postwar era, when economic depressions were banished but unemployment was not expelled along with them. And it is lacking today, when neoliberal policies have weakened core worker rights, while policy makers stabilize prices on the backs of the unemployed. The Job Guarantee is a policy that was needed well before we irreversibly polluted the environment, and it is one that will still be necessary after we have cleaned it up.

The vision for the green Job Guarantee articulated here connects job creation to environmental conservation. It also defines *green policies* as those that address all forms of waste and devastation, including and especially those of our human resources. A green policy must remedy the neglect and squander that come with economic distress, unemployment, and precarious work in particular. As the late Nobel Prize winning economist William Vickrey argued, unemployment is "at best equivalent to vandalism," bringing an unconscionable toll and ruin on individuals, families, and communities.[2] Yet conventional wisdom considers unemployment to be "normal." Economists even call it "natural" and devise policies around some "optimal" level of joblessness.

The idea that involuntary unemployment is an unfortunate but unavoidable occurrence, and that there is an appropriate level of unemployment necessary for the smooth functioning of the economy, is among the great, unexamined myths of our time. It is also bad economics.

To make the case for the Job Guarantee policy, the book begins with a thought experiment before moving on to the diagnosis and economic analysis. It asks the reader to imagine what the Job Guarantee policy might look like in very practical terms and the impact it might have on unemployed people and their families. We consider under what circumstances someone might need to access the program and what kinds of projects could ensure that they would always walk out of the unemployment office with a basic living-wage job offer.

The reason for this approach is that unemployment has become far too abstract and paradoxically impersonal. Few things are as personal as losing one's job, and yet most economists and policy makers talk about unemployment much like meteorologists talk about the weather. Unemployment is treated as if it were a natural occurrence, about which governments can do little beyond providing temporary protection like unemployment insurance. Millions might have to endure joblessness as the economy slogs through a prolonged recession, but when the weather clears unemployment will dissipate again. Still, the inevitable drumbeat of globalization and technological change dictates that some people will necessarily stay (structurally) unemployed. Or so the story goes.

Unemployment is thus de-personified and internalized as a tolerable natural occurrence in a globalized world. It has become common to personify it only when unemployed people are blamed for their own lot – another myth this book aims to debunk. When economic conditions are favorable, unemployment and poverty are often believed to be the result of poor initiative (jobseekers have not upgraded their skills), or some other individual moral failing (substance abuse, criminal record, "bad choices" of one kind or another). Unemployment is thereby reanimated, but not humanized.

Some readers may share this view and it is hoped that this book will change their minds. Even in the best of times, decent job opportunities are in short supply for a great many people, due to stacked circumstances beyond their control. The consequences are devastating, yet largely avoidable. The questions I want to raise are these: What if we devised a system that – rain or shine, "moral failings" or not – guaranteed job opportunities to anyone who wanted to work, irrespective of their experience, training, or personal situation? What would such an economy look like? Would the sky fall? Would it create economic conditions and consequences worse than the ones we already face? Or would it usher in a great many benefits that we may not have considered before? Would a world with a public option for jobs be any worse than one in which even the "good economy" leaves millions without decent employment? Or would it provide a new basis for economic security and stability?

To begin answering these questions, Chapter 1 makes a very simple proposal: to ensure that the unemployment offices (the so-called American Job Centers) begin to act as genuine employment offices that provide living-wage public service employment opportunities on demand.

Chapter 2 documents the many catch-22 situations unemployed people face in the labor market. It challenges us to think of the right to a job in the same way we think of the right to retirement security or the right to primary and secondary education. Modern fine-tuning policies (both monetary and fiscal) that treat unemployment as "natural" and "unavoidable" perpetrate the above-mentioned vandalism on people, communities, and the environment. Once we take into account its social, economic, and environmental costs, it becomes clear that unemployment is already "paid for" and the price tag is high.

Chapter 3 argues that guaranteeing employment represents a new social contract and macroeconomic stabilization policy that falls within a long tradition of government guarantees. By combining key features of other public options and price support schemes, the Job Guarantee would have transformative effects on the economy. It would establish a new labor standard with an uncompromising living-wage floor for all working people, while stabilizing employment, inflation, and government spending more effectively than current practice. It would also replace, once and for all, unemployment as an economic stabilizer. The chapter enumerates the other benefits of the Job Guarantee, including but not limited to its impact on state budgets, inequality, service sector employment, and the lives of those who do not seek paid work.

Addressing the question of cost, Chapter 4 provides the reader with a new perspective on affordability, and sheds light on why most guarantees are usually provided by the federal government. This chapter considers the economic meaning of the term "the power of the public purse," and separates the *real* from the *financial* costs, as well as the *real resource constraints* from the *artificial financial constraints*. It also provides estimates of the size of the Job Guarantee budget and presents the results from a macroeconomic simulation of the program's impact on the US economy.

Chapter 5 turns to the question of implementation and design and explains how the proposal offered here differs from others. It illustrates why the Job Guarantee is inherently *green*, and provides examples of specific projects that could be developed and managed using a decentralized and participatory model. It recommends that the Job Guarantee is organized as a National Care Act that prioritizes care for the environment, care for the people, and care for the communities. The chapter also addresses some frequently asked questions and highlights important lessons from similar real-world job creation programs.

The concluding Chapter 6 evaluates the program's overwhelming popularity and symbiotic relationship with the Green New Deal. It clarifies the different uses of "guaranteeing jobs" that can be found in the climate discourse and situates the Job Guarantee proposal within the green agenda. It also explains why the Job Guarantee would still be needed in a zero-emissions world where temperatures have stabilized, and concludes with some thoughts about its role and place in the international policy architecture.

1

A Public Option for Good Jobs

It took eleven long years after the Great Financial Crisis to bring the US unemployment rate to a post-war low of 3.5 percent. Still there were millions of people who could not find paid work. The official figure in February 2020 was 5.8 million, but with a proper count that number would be more than doubled.[1] Job loss is not an affliction that touches everyone equally. It disproportionately affects the young, the poor, individuals with disabilities, people of color, veterans, and former inmates.

Growth, we are told, will raise all boats, but drawn-out jobless recoveries have been the norm for half a century now, and jobs have increasingly failed to deliver good pay. When we consider the question "When the economy grows, who gains?" we find a disturbing answer. In the immediate postwar era, as economies expanded after each recession, the vast

Figure 1 Distribution of Average Income Growth During Expansions

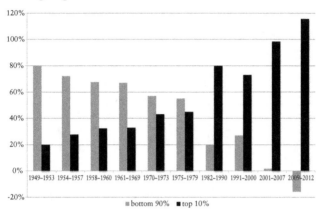

Source: Pavlina R. Tcherneva, "Reorienting Fiscal Policy: A Bottom-up Approach," *Journal of Post Keynesian Economics*, 37(1), 2014: 43–66.

majority of the gains went to the bottom 90 percent of families. The exact opposite has been true of the last four expansions (Figure 1).[2] Since the 1980s, a growing economy primarily grew the incomes of the wealthiest 10 percent of families. Worse, during the recovery from the Great Recession, average real incomes for the bottom 90 percent of families *fell* in the first three years of the expansion.

Today, millions of people cannot find paid work, and millions more need above-poverty pay. Wages have stagnated for decades. Real average income for the bottom 90 percent of families was $34,580

Table 1 Runaway Inequality

Real Average Income (excl. capital gains)	Bottom 90%	Top 10%	Top 1%	Top 0.01%
1997	$35,357	$227,843	$806,585	$11,986,014
2017	$34,580	$282,921	$1,075,058	$19,235,681
Percent change	−2.2%	24.2%	33.3%	60.5%

Source: Author's tabulations of T. Piketty and E. Saez, "Income Inequality in the United States, 1913–1998," *Quarterly Journal of Economics*, 118(1), 2019 [2003]: 1–39.

in 2017, 2.2 percent *lower* than it was twenty years earlier. Meanwhile, real average income of the richest 0.01 percent of families grew by 60.5 percent during the same period (Table 1), and was nearly 556 times higher than that of the bottom 90 percent (or 1,000 times higher if we include capital gains).[3]

Behind the unemployment and inequality numbers hide the millions of different faces, experiences, circumstances, and personal challenges of those dealing with joblessness and inadequate pay.

Maybe you are one of them or you know someone who is. Maybe you lost your job in the Great Recession and are now working two part-time jobs, struggling to pay the bills. Maybe you graduated high school, cannot afford college, and are looking to save some money first. Maybe the children have fled the nest and you, the stay-at-home parent, would like to find paid work, but it has been decades since your last job and you don't know where to begin. Maybe you've sent out 215 résumés already,[4] but even in this "strong economy" you still cannot find stable well-paid work. Maybe it's because of your age, gender, the color of your skin, or your criminal record. Maybe you are someone with a disability who wishes to work, but getting the kind of jobs you could do seems impossible and, if you do get one, the current law allows your employer to pay you as little as $1/hour.[5] Maybe the firm found a "better" candidate. You keep knocking on the next door, emailing the next employer, but the call never comes.

The unemployment office is here to help – you take additional classes, spruce up your résumé, and practice your interview skills. You put your best foot forward but strike out again. Or maybe you are hired, but it's only another low-paying job with no benefits. You barely make ends meet and the long commute and unpredictable shifts make coming home for dinner or doing homework with the kids a challenge.

You are willing to work hard for that job, but the job just isn't working for you. And this time you are lucky. Remember 2009, the overcrowded unemployment offices, and the many online ads that said: "the unemployed need not apply"?[6]

But maybe you are none of the above people. Maybe you have an OK job, at least compared to your friends. The pay is not great but the firm promises opportunities for advancement. You can provide for the family and, after a few more months, you will finally earn that two-week paid vacation. The only problem is that your boss harasses you mercilessly. But you stick around. Could you really give up this "stable" job? And you are so close. You can almost smell the ocean.

Maybe you live in Puerto Rico, and your shop was swept away by Hurricane Maria. Many people died, many more fled, and a year and a half later one in twelve people on the island were still looking for work. Or maybe you escaped the California fires, but you lost your job and the FEMA money for your incinerated home is running out. You and many others in flood- and tornado-ravaged areas still need to pay the bills, and local communities still need rebuilding.

How many of these stories can we tell? In the US – millions; globally – hundreds of millions. The loss of one's job and livelihood is not just a consequence of unusual circumstances or "acts of God." It is a regular occurrence. The drumbeat of the economy, expanding in good times and shrinking in bad, along with outsourcing and technological change, creates ongoing job losses. And while new employment opportunities are also created, they are never enough for all jobseekers even at the peak of expansions. Meanwhile many workers are in unstable, poorly paid jobs. In 2018, there were 6.9 million working people earning below the official poverty level.[7] For millions of Americans, one job is just not enough.

What if we changed all that and made it a social and economic objective that no jobseeker would be left without (at a minimum) decent living-wage work? What would be the impact on the lives of people, communities, and the economy?

Imagine that you go back to the unemployment office but this time, in addition to every other resource it offers, it also produces a list of local public service jobs, each offering a basic wage (say $15/hour), healthcare, and affordable quality childcare. You can choose from full- and part-time options. As it does now, the office continues to offer additional wraparound services including training, credentialing, GED completion, family-focused case management, transportation subsidies, counseling, referrals, and others.

These are local job opportunities in the municipality or local non-profits (finally, a shorter commute), but they are federally funded (not that you care, a paycheck is a paycheck). The urban fishery is starting a new STEM program with local schools. The historical society is digitizing its maps and records. The Green New Deal has launched a comprehensive weatherization program and green infrastructure projects abound. A project is hiring for that water-pipe replacement that dragged on for years, and the cleanup of the vacant lot behind the municipal park needs workers. Local community groups are running outreach programs for veterans, the homeless, at-risk youths, and former inmates, and community health clinics are offering apprenticeships and training opportunities. A community theater is running afterschool programs for children and evening classes for adults.

All of these jobs were either nonexistent or the projects were sorely understaffed before the Job Guarantee was launched. If your community has been battered by extreme weather disasters or environmental hazards, the program will help staff the cleanup and rebuilding efforts and the region's revitalized fire and flood prevention programs. And this entire menu of options is organized and supplied courtesy of the Job Guarantee. It is a program in cooperation with local and municipal governments and local non-profit providers to ensure that no jobseeker is ever turned away.

A Public Option for Good Jobs

The Job Guarantee office is there to help you transition to better-paid employment opportunities in the private or public sectors. The economy is growing and new job ads promise opportunities for advancement, flexible hours, and telecommuting. With your additional experience and training, you line up some job offers. You say goodbye to the Job Guarantee and are off to the next opportunity.

Or maybe you do not need the Job Guarantee at all. After all, you are a highly educated and skilled individual with an entirely different professional experience – your career ladder is clear, your contacts are many, and you are able to jump from one opportunity to the next with ease. You earn a good income, provide for your family, and would never consider or likely need to apply for the Job Guarantee. But the program has helped rehabilitate your neighborhood, built community gardens in your kids' schools, organized new programs and community events in the local library, and restored the nearby hiking trails and public beaches.

Can this become a realistic scenario? Can we put in place a program that provides a basic employment safety net for those who need it, while creating some much needed community work that benefits everyone in every state and every county, no matter how small or how remote? Subsequent chapters will argue that the answer is yes, and that we already know a lot about how to make it happen. Such a program would deliver overwhelming benefits – economic, social, and environmental.

Maybe these stories resonate and you can see the impact a public job option could have. With the Job Guarantee, you could find local work in a community project that mattered to you. You could say "no" to an abusive employer if you had a living-wage alternative. You could get a starter job before moving on to other opportunities, and save yourself the frustration of being rejected time and again by employers who may not like your sparse résumé. You would be able to avoid the stress of applying for food stamps and other government programs, because you have a living-wage job and can make ends meet. We are here just scratching the surface of the difference a Job Guarantee could make to the lives of the millions of people behind the unemployment and underemployment numbers.

But maybe these stories don't resonate. It just sounds too good to be true. Isn't there something called the "natural unemployment rate"? What can the government really do about it? Can it even create jobs and, if it tried, wouldn't it distort market incentives? Maybe you worry that people wouldn't work as hard if they weren't afraid of being unemployed.

Or that the program would ruin productivity. And how much would it cost? Isn't it very expensive to hire millions of people? All of these concerns and more are addressed in the following pages.

The economics of unemployment is bad economics. One need not share the personal distress unemployed people and their families face to understand that hiring those willing to work is a much better economic approach than the one we have at present. Reaching that understanding is the task of the next chapter.

2

A Steep Price for a
Broken Status Quo

The economics of employment is straightforward: a person will find a job if someone is willing to hire them. Typically, we think of firms doing all the hiring because they comprise about 80 percent of total employment in the US. And firm hiring depends on profitability. If customers are walking in the door, cash registers are ringing, and profits are rising, then firms will hire. And when sales and profits decline, mass layoffs result. But about a fifth of all jobs are created not for monetary gain, per se, but in order to meet some specific public purpose. Roads must be maintained, schools must be staffed, food and drugs must be inspected, security and justice must be provided. Non-profit, local, state, and federal government employment is devoted to serving the broader public interest. The argument put forth here is that hiring the involuntarily unemployed serves an important public purpose of its own – one that has been neglected largely because unemployment has been accepted as unavoidable and, even worse, as necessary for economic stability.

How "Natural" is Unemployment?

Suppose you heard that, in a strong economy, the optimal level of children who wanted to but were unable to receive primary and secondary education was 5 percent; or that there was a natural level of starvation equal to 5 percent of the population; or that 5 percent of people would ideally remain without shelter. Modern societies have arrived at the moral position that policy should do all it can to eradicate illiteracy, hunger, and homelessness. Without question, we can and must do much better in doing so, but we do not *design* or *implement* policy on the basis that there is some "optimal" level for these social ills. Our aspirations and ethical commitments are to guarantee access to schooling, food, and shelter to all.

And yet economists regularly talk about unemployment in these terms – as something that is not only inevitable, but also necessary for the smooth functioning of the economy – and formulate policies on the premise that there is a "natural" level of unemployment. This was succinctly put by Federal Reserve Chairman Jerome Powell in January 2019: "We need the concept of a natural rate of unemployment. We need to have some sense of whether unemployment is high, low, or *just right*."[1]

What is the "right" number of people who are struggling to find paid work? Many economists fear that if unemployment is "too low" and labor markets are "too tight" then firms will have to raise wages to attract workers and in turn raise prices to recover those costs. Low unemployment, the argument goes, could cause high or even accelerating inflation, producing one of the clunkiest concepts in economics – the Non-Accelerating Inflation Rate of Unemployment (NAIRU).

Inflation-fighting central banks then aim to fine-tune the economy around the NAIRU.[2] Countless think tanks, academics, and government institutions spend valuable resources on trying to identify this elusive "optimal level" of unemployment, while the actual number of unemployed people yo-yos around as the economy grows and slows down. The Congressional Budget Office (CBO) has maintained that the "natural level" throughout the postwar era was between 4.5 and 6.5 percent, and yet here we are today with official unemployment at 3.5 percent.

A Steep Price for a Broken Status Quo

It is no consolation that Chairman Powell recently admitted, under oath, that the unemployment–inflation relationship has collapsed.[3] The search for the NAIRU continues. Top economists vigorously defend it and the Fed's explicit objective is to manage inflation by slowing down the rate of investment and hiring when unemployment gets "too low."[4]

The trouble with this fine-tuning approach is threefold. First, the NAIRU is a myth.[5] Economists (and the Fed) cannot figure out the nature of the unemployment–inflation relationship, nor whether it is even a causal one.[6] Second, on its own admission, the Fed has no reliable theory of inflation either.[7] Third, despite failing to pin down the NAIRU or the inflation target, Fed officials have been insisting at least since 2014 that the economy has reached full employment. Many will remember a similar experience in the 1990s, when experts kept warning that the economy has reached maximum employment, even as the unemployment rate kept breaking through every new official NAIRU estimate, with no accelerating inflation in sight. And like a scene from *Groundhog Day*, with NAIRU warnings on repeat, the unemployed people are caught in a jobless trap with no way out.

This problem is worse around the world. In 2012, the Annual Economic Forecast of the

European Commission claimed that the natural rate of unemployment in Spain was 26.6 percent – the economy simply could not do better. And yet it did. As unemployment fell (granted, insufficiently) from its depression levels, the commission kept revising down its own NAIRU estimates. It is hard not to conclude that the NAIRU has provided cover for the profound policy failure of tackling unemployment head on.

This was not always the view from the Fed. In 1945, the Board of Governors put together a comprehensive report on the maintenance of full employment, production and living standards during the transition from a wartime to a peacetime economy, arguing that the "two evils [unemployment and inflation] . . . will not cancel out [and] both must be prevented." The Fed outlined a sweeping long-term program for full employment and price stability that included a series of measures, among which the "Guarantee of Employment" was considered *"perhaps the most essential part of the concept of a national minimum standard."*[8] The Fed argued that this guarantee was "the first clause in a bill of economic rights," and that a "fuller and better utilization of our resources, human and material, for the benefit of all" was a central national economic *goal* of the Federal Reserve itself.[9]

The Fed's approach could not be more different today. Unemployment is sanctioned by government policy. The NAIRU has been used to rationalize policy responses that permit the deliberate slowing down of the economy and the increase of joblessness to tame inflationary pressures, thus reinforcing the existence of much economic hardship. But unemployment is not at all unavoidable, and direct measures to wipe it out are the superior policy option. Before we reckon with the high costs of the status quo, however, we need to address another pervasive myth – the idea that jobs are abundant and unemployment is an individual failure.

The Labor Market: A Catch-22 for Many

It is a common view that in a strong economy anyone who looks for work will be able to find it. Any difficulties they might have must therefore be due to some personal shortcoming – a lack of required skills, inadequate education, or poor incentives and decision making. Of course, for most economists "full employment" actually refers to a situation where millions of people are involuntarily out of work (whether through personal failings or not), not to a situation where anyone who is ready,

Figure 2 Chronic Job Shortages

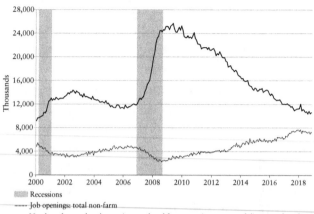

Source: Author's calculations based on data from the US Bureau of Labor Statistics.

willing, and able to work could actually secure a job.

In reality, even if one makes all the "right" decisions, the labor market is not a fair game. Even at the peak of an expansion, there are always more jobseekers than there are job openings (Figure 2). For many people the labor market is riddled with paradoxical catch-22 situations. The for-profit sector creates the vast majority of employment opportunities, but it is not in the business of hiring everyone who wants to work. As noted, firms hire staff when their sales and profits justify it, but there are many other reasons (apart from deficient sales) why they never employ all of the unemployed.

First, firms do not *like* to hire unemployed people, and especially the long-term unemployed.[10] They prefer to hire people who are already working or have smaller gaps in their work experience. For the unemployed, this is a catch-22. During the Great Recession, as we noted above, some job ads even warned: "the unemployed need not apply" (a practice that was challenged in US courts).[11] Furthermore, firms are reluctant to hire long-term unemployed people because they consider nine months of unemployment to be equivalent to four years of lost work experience.[12]

For many, the mark of unemployment is their main obstacle to securing a good job. Firms try to avoid the "risk" of hiring and training them, which produces a modern paradox: an economy in which millions are seeking work, while firms fret over finding qualified workers. This paradox is made worse by the fact that, as the economy grows, firms tighten their hiring criteria.[13] This means that those who need to find work the most – the long-term unemployed – are precisely those facing the highest barriers to entry. Not only are they hired last and fired first – and so unable to build up sufficient work experience, gain job tenure, or grow their incomes – they are also most likely to be locked out of employment opportunities altogether when employers change the rules of the game. It is another catch-22.

Training and education do not resolve this paradox, though they may shuffle people around on the unemployment line. Over the last few decades, higher education has delivered soaring student loans, but not the jobs and incomes to pay them off. Like a Sisyphean boulder, crushing student debt has meant that young people are not able to afford a home, get married, or retain enough discretionary income, putting the brakes on economic growth. Another catch-22.

Even with training programs private firms have other criteria (visible and invisible) for exclusion. Discrimination on the basis of gender, race, age, and sex are well documented. Stay-at-home parents are about half as likely to receive a second interview as unemployed parents, and only about one-third as likely as employed parents.[14] African American applicants without a criminal record are called back with an offer of a job or a second interview less frequently than white applicants *with* a criminal record.[15] People with disabilities are systematically locked out of employment opportunities and have been the last group to see their employment rates reach pre-crisis levels.[16]

Figure 3 Unemployment: The Human Yo-Yo

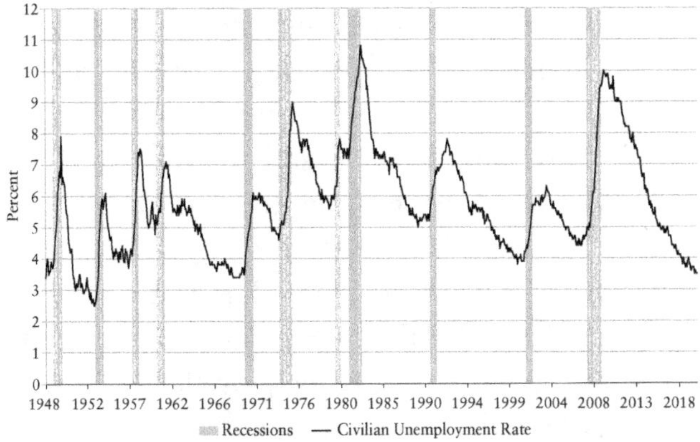

Source: US Bureau of Labor Statistics.

The Human Yo-Yo Effect

All of these challenges in the labor market, coupled with an economy that regularly lays off millions of people during recessions, have created a human yo-yo effect (Figure 3). Unemployment in the US is extremely volatile: it starts with an avalanche of mass layoffs in recessions, but recoveries are slow and anemic. Jobless recoveries have been accepted as normal and unavoidable. In the meantime, the share of long-term unemployment in total unemployment has steadily risen since the 1960s. Unemployment, in a sense, creates unemployability.

The labor market is a cruel game of musical chairs. In fact it is worse, because many unemployed people cannot find a chair (i.e., paid work), and if they do (especially in the low-wage sectors), they are often discriminated against, harassed, subject to wage theft, and under constant threat of losing their jobs and benefits.

There are not enough jobs, but there are not enough *good* jobs either. The policy of maintaining a reserve pool of the unemployed, the stacked obstacles the jobless face in the labor market, and the human yo-yo effect of mass layoffs, all inflict high costs on society and the economy.

Unemployment is Expensive

Just like we do not talk about the "optimal level" of homelessness or illiteracy, the notion of "optimal unemployment" would not survive long if economists took full account of its social and economic costs. A wealth of research from psychology, the cognitive sciences, and public health indicates that the costs of unemployment, poorly paid employment, unstable and erratic employment, and involuntary part-time employment are simply staggering. This suggests that we should think of unemployment and precarious employment as a disease – at once vicious, chronic, and deadly.

What one will not see by looking at the official numbers is that unemployment spreads like a virus. To get a sense of how it moves, it is useful to observe an animated geographical map of unemployment over time.[17] The first thing one notices is that persistent joblessness (often in the double digits even during economic booms) does not just plague the Rust Belt and the Appalachian Mountains, but also affects countless communities from the Sierra Nevada to the Colorado Plains, the Coast Ranges, and the Deep South.

The second notable feature is that unemployment presents an unmistakable contagion effect. Imagine throwing a pebble into water – the initial shock creates ripples that move further and further away. This is what happens with unemployment. When recessions hit, mass layoffs in distressed areas spread and multiply like a disease from community to community. The loss of income and jobs causes those who have been laid off to drastically reduce their spending, which impacts neighboring businesses, who respond in turn by laying off other workers. And on and on it goes. In a sense, one unemployed person throws another one out of work. Unemployment spreads like a disease in recessions,

33

while in expansions it lingers in the epicenters of these outbreaks, creating chronic economic distress. Figure 4 gives a snapshot of the situation after the Great Recession, showing double-digit unemployment rates across the country well into the recovery, something one cannot see by looking only at the official aggregate unemployment statistics.

The metaphor of a deadly epidemic is apt. Without slipping into hyperbole, unemployment is literally deadly. Widely cited research by Case and Deaton[18] found that increased mortality among working-class white men has been driven by "deaths of despair" resulting from the pain, distress, and social dysfunction following the loss of stable blue-collar work that began in the 1970s and continued well after the Great Recession. Economic insecurity and unemployment in particular have produced complex socioeconomic and health problems that have contributed to the rise in mortality, but the link between unemployment and dying is even more direct.

A metadata analysis of sixty-three countries found that one in five suicides are due to unemployment – an impact that is nine times higher than previously believed.[19] Another panel study of twenty-five OECD countries supports these findings.[20] Stuckler and Basu similarly find that, since the Great

Figure 4 Unemployment During the Great Recession and Beyond

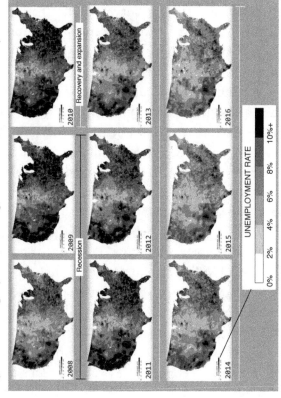

Source: FlowingData, "Animated Map of Unemployment," October 16, 2016.

35

Recession, areas with higher unemployment rates experience higher suicide rates.[21] Other research reports that long-term unemployment is associated with higher mortality twenty years after the spell of unemployment.[22] For survivors and their families, unemployment is extremely costly. But it brings large costs to the wider economy as well.

The unemployed suffer a *permanent* loss of lifetime earnings[23] and incur significant health costs – they are sicker, make more trips to the doctor, and spend more on medication. They have higher rates of alcoholism, physical illness, depression, and anxiety.[24] This is the case around the world as well, according to a metadata study that examined several variables of mental health, including mixed symptoms of distress, depression, anxiety, psychosomatic symptoms, subjective wellbeing, and self esteem.[25] All of these combined and complex health effects create a vicious cycle that makes it harder for unemployed people to reenter the labor market.[26]

Joblessness, it turns out, is *its own* catch-22 – creating the difficult personal and health conditions that prevent a person from escaping it. This paradox is made worse by the fact that unemployment drastically and permanently reduces a person's social capital and participation,[27] cutting them off from social networks and relations that are, for many, the bridge to re-employment. The isolation that unemployment brings is compounded by other well-documented scarring effects, such as a permanent decline in wellbeing, which linger even after a person has been reemployed. One study found that, of the total costs of unemployment, the non-monetary costs are between 85 and 93 percent, overwhelming the costs of a permanent loss of income.[28] This suggests that policies which mainly focus on providing income to the unemployed would be inadequate.

It should not come as a surprise – though it is altogether ignored by the research on the "natural rate" – that unemployment harms not just those who have lost their jobs but also their families. Unemployment is among the causes of malnutrition, growth stunting, mental health problems, poor educational and labor market outcomes, and reduced social mobility of spouses and children.[29] In the US, children experience the highest poverty rate and 80 percent of poor children live in a family without a working adult.

Unemployment contributes to the entrenched urban blight and economic destitution in many communities and is a factor in violent and property crimes.[30] Youth unemployment, crime, and right-wing extremism are strongly correlated.[31] Globally, many countries are experiencing obstinate depression levels of youth unemployment – a ticking time bomb of social problems.[32] In the US, unemployment among formerly incarcerated individuals is more than five times the national rate, higher than in the worst years of the Great Depression, while unemployment is a major factor in recidivism.[33]

Beyond the personal costs, there are also broader macroeconomic impacts of unemployment. It increases the general level of income inequality in most countries,[34] and produces social exclusion that exacerbates interracial and interethnic tensions.[35] It has a negative impact on technological change, innovation, and output, and is a contributing factor to financial crises and economic instability,[36] as well as to social and political instability, human trafficking, forced and child labor, exploitation, and slavery.

As if that were not enough, unemployment also depresses economic growth. In the midst of the Great Recession, according to one estimate, the US economy lost $10 billion of output *each day* as a result of high levels of unemployment.[37] (For comparison purposes, this amount is equivalent to the *annual* budget of the Environmental Protection Agency for 2016.) Even at the peak of the expansion in 2007, when unemployment was relatively low, the daily GDP loss from unemployment was around $500 million.

In other words, we give up millions of dollars of goods and services every day, while carrying the enormous personal, social, and economic costs of unemployment, because we have accepted it as natural, unavoidable, and necessary.

Unemployment is already paid for. We forfeit the social and economic value we could generate by eradicating it, while carrying its real and financial costs. It is a global problem with global implications. It is a cancer – linked to the gradual ruin of communities, the collapse of the social fabric, the opioid epidemic, poor child health and education outcomes, overcrowded prisons, mental and health deterioration, to name just a few of its overwhelming effects. These are unnecessary costs. Most of them could be avoided with a program that guarantees a basic living-wage job to all.

A Broken Status Quo: Policy Responses

Even central banks with a dual mandate prioritize fighting inflation over fighting unemployment. And if the policy priorities were reversed, there is little reason to believe they could pin the unemployment rate at the "desirable" level, much less create conditions where anyone who sought work could find it. What central banks could do for the labor market is adopt a do-no-harm approach, abandon the NAIRU, and stop pumping the brakes on the economy in order to slow job growth. As the next chapter will make clear, there are no economic, social, or moral reasons for using the unemployed as a bulwark against inflation.

Fiscal policy hasn't done a good job of tackling unemployment either, even though it has more tools at its disposal. It was demoted in the post-Reagan era and paired with deregulation, wage suppression, and trickle-down policies that masqueraded as sound economic policy. The result was the greatest transfer of wealth to the top and the slowest payroll employment recovery rates in the postwar era. But the earlier postwar "Keynesian" fiscal policies did not do the trick either. Government stimulus policies failed to generate the conditions that would ensure a job for every jobseeker. Traditional fiscal pump priming typically prioritizes stabilizing investment over stabilizing employment (the latter being regarded merely as a byproduct of the former). This is done via loan guarantees or contracts with guaranteed profits, subsidies, and bailouts. Indeed, fiscal policies often help stabilize and *increase* corporate profits *in the midst of a recession*, whereas jobless recoveries have become the norm. By contrast, the Job Guarantee is a straightforward response: the policy solution to someone unable to find paid work is to provide them with an employment opportunity.

Today, a guaranteed retirement income and public education have become fundamental components of the policy landscape. And just as we do not target either some "natural rate" of retirees who are uninsured or a certain illiteracy rate, it makes little sense to target a given rate of involuntary unemployment. In a sense, the government chooses the unemployment rate by insisting that the NAIRU must serve as a policy guide. Even the presumed benefits of managing inflation by taming changes in demand do not justify keeping people out of work. As the next chapter will explain, the Job Guarantee replaces the NAIRU with a powerful automatic stabilizer that delivers full employment and price stability. It also brings a range of economic and social benefits without inflicting the unbearable costs of unemployment on society.

3

The Job Guarantee:
A New Social Contract
and Macroeconomic Model

How does one raise the roof without first securing the floor? This was the question behind FDR's Economic Bill of Rights, the Civil Rights March on Washington for Jobs and Freedom, and the Green New Deal's insistence that a green transformation requires basic economic security for all.

The more affluent an economy becomes, argued the late John Kenneth Galbraith, the more repugnant the idea that some people get to enjoy the fruits of their labor, while others are left behind without employment. And while the right to a good job was not guaranteed in practice during the Golden Age of the American economy, it was at least common to defend it. Presidential addresses – Democrat or Republican – echoed it, while advocating for strengthening labor conditions and using public service for unemployment relief. These ideas and vocabulary were expunged in the post-Reagan era, when the triumph of market fundamentalism wreaked havoc on jobs and incomes. Prosperity for working families was no longer a government goal. Economic security and wellbeing was the domain of the few. So methodical and effective was the assault on labor and employment conditions that even some voices from the left (the traditional champions of working families) had all but given up on the ambition to guarantee this fundamental right to all.

The surrender was accelerated by orthodox economists' insistence that markets should set all prices – including the price of labor – and that the natural rate of unemployment should serve as the bulwark against inflation. The ideological turn was complete, labor and full employment were abandoned, and the very popular idea of a living-wage floor was severely undermined. The rise of monetarism and the mythical NAIRU provided the perfect cover for sacrificing jobs on the altar of price stability.

None of this was rooted in good economics. Business enterprises and governments set most prices – the former with increasingly vast market power and the latter with the power of the public purse. This was well understood in the immediate postwar era when the government budgetary and regulatory apparatus was the primary inflation-management tool. Few self-respecting economists and policy makers argued that unemployment was necessary to fight inflation (Friedrich Hayek and Milton Friedman were notable exceptions). The dominant narrative during the Golden Age was that the government was responsible for providing a basic labor standard – from pay and working conditions to national labor relations.

But without the right to decent employment, the foundations on which early labor laws were built were weak. The threat of the sack loomed in every negotiation between unions and firms; it justified job outsourcing and the hiring of cheap migrant labor, broke the postwar social contract, eroded workplace solidarity, and was used to bust unions themselves. The threat of unemployment remained forever the most powerful tool firms had over their workers.

The Job Guarantee is the missing piece of the Roosevelt Revolution. By securing a fundamental economic right, it would usher in a new social contract pledging that unemployment and poorly paid employment would no longer be used for the purposes of presumed economic stabilization. Like every major policy of the past, it too would bring significant structural changes to the economy, the most significant of which would be forever exiling the NAIRU from the economic policy kit. As a major macroeconomic policy, the Job Guarantee would provide the countercyclical economic stabilization that unemployment currently serves. As a policy that guarantees a basic job at a basic wage, it would provide a minimum labor standard for all jobs in the economy, including an uncompromising living-wage floor with potentially far-reaching benefits for all people – working or not. As a permanent feature of the safety net, it would act as a critical preventative policy, foiling a range of social and economic ills and labor market problems. As the cornerstone of a revived Economic Bill of Rights and the green agenda, it would be an instrument for tackling pressing social and economic problems.

Guarantees All Around: Public Options and Price Supports

While folklore tells us that there are no guarantees in life, in fact guarantees are everywhere. Most are provided courtesy of the public sector. Some are universal, while others are conditional. Public education, public libraries, public safety, public defenders are just a few universal guarantees. Social Security ensures a retirement income subject to some minimum earning history, though people with disabilities and non-working spouses are also covered. Guarantees extend not only to families but to corporations as well. Contracts with guaranteed profits are widespread globally, often benefitting defense, transportation, and high-tech industries. So are loan guarantees (explicit or implicit) where the government promises to assume the debt of a borrower in trouble (with the 2008 financial bailout as the most extravagant postwar example). Bank deposits are guaranteed via deposit insurance up to a certain amount, and a plethora of government programs around the world guarantee minimum prices for farm commodities.

Some of these guarantees come via public options, others via good-old-fashioned government price supports. With public options, the government directly provides the essential good or service to ensure universal access (e.g., public schools, public roads, public safety). With price supports, it guarantees that the price of a good or service never falls below a certain level (e.g., bank deposits or some agricultural commodities).

The Job Guarantee has the features of a public option and the benefits of a price support scheme. As a public option, it guarantees universal but *voluntary* access to a basic public service employment opportunity to anyone who wants one.[1] It is similar to the way individuals are guaranteed a public defender if they choose not to hire a private one, or the way families are guaranteed a seat in a public school even if they opt to send their kids to a private school instead. Since the Job Guarantee provides a fixed base wage, it also serves as a price support policy, not only for workers in the program, but also for all workers in the economy. This is because it acts as an alternative to the most undesirable private sector jobs – those with poor pay, abuse, harassment, wage theft, dangerous workplaces, and other problems – thereby establishing the minimum required pay and working conditions for all employers to meet.

Price Supports, Buffer Stocks, and Living Wages

The notion that an essential resource in the economy – working people – should enjoy some form of a guarantee and price support is hardly a radical proposition. We do it regularly and effectively for all sorts of inputs of production, as a matter of both principle and economic efficiency. One may think of the minimum wage as the price floor for workers but, without the guarantee of employment, it is not entirely effective. So long as there is a shortage of jobs, the wage of the person who cannot secure a minimum-wage employment opportunity is, in fact, zero.

Consider how price supports work for agricultural commodities. Governments around the world have employed a range of methods for setting and stabilizing commodity prices. Often this was done via so-called buffer stock programs,[2] where the government would purchase the surplus production of the commodity (say corn) at a predetermined price when demand suddenly fell, and then release it for sale from storage once demand for the commodity recovered.[3] Buffer stock programs have the effect of ensuring that the price of the commodity does not fall below the government-administered price. By purchasing the surplus and selling it when there is market shortage, the government both employs the commodity (i.e., ensures that no bushel of corn goes unsold) and maintains its price floor.

When it comes to employment, the government has instituted a federal minimum wage, but not a comparable program for purchasing the surplus, so to speak, i.e., for employing the unemployed. This means that the government price support policy (the minimum wage) is rather weak, as it does not extend to the unemployed. To establish a robust wage floor, the government needs *both* a fixed base wage policy *and* a policy that would employ the unemployed on standby at that predetermined wage.

The Job Guarantee would act as an employment buffer stock scheme with the added benefit that it stabilizes the wage floor, overall prices, and the economy as a whole. Mass layoffs in recessions depress worker wages and total demand, putting downward pressure on all prices. By employing the unemployed, the public option would maintain full employment at living wages, ensuring a much more robust floor to collapsing aggregate demand than in conditions of chronic unemployment. When the economy recovers and firms resume hiring, workers would transition from the Job Guarantee program into private sector employment. Government spending and payrolls would shrink, relieving any potential inflationary pressures from private sector hiring and the increased demand. This countercyclical feature of the program, offsetting changes in private sector demand for workers, would stabilize both economic and price fluctuations and could be strengthened by training, credentialing, and other efforts to transition Job Guarantee workers to better-paid employment opportunities. In other words, the Job Guarantee would provide an *economy-wide living-wage*

49

floor, *true full employment*, and a powerful *shock absorber* for the economy.

Setting the Most Important Price

There is another buffer stock program of the past that almost everyone knows – that of gold. Recall that, under a gold standard, a nation pegs its currency to given ounces of gold. Under such a monetary system, the government effectively sets a fixed price for gold and buys or sells it at that price, whenever private demand for gold drops or increases, respectively. In other words, the government uses a buffer stock mechanism to ensure the full employment and price stability of gold!

It is indefensible on both economic and moral grounds to have run full employment and price support programs for agricultural commodities or gold, without doing the same for jobseekers. Working people, for reasons that should be obvious, need a robust price support more than any other commodity. This was recognized as far back as Adam Smith, who argued that labor must, at a minimum, be paid a subsistence wage – an idea that has evolved into the modern living-wage concept. Working people need enforceable wage laws, but they also need the *assurance* of an accessible living-wage job option.

Grain commodities and gold have enjoyed price supports, even as they have no demands over the level of their pay.[4] For most people, living incomes and family-sustaining wages are essential for survival. Nor do commodities "care" about the conditions of their employment. They may be stored in silos, left to rot unsold, or locked up in a vault, but individuals and their families experience the mental and physical toll of joblessness and poorly paid employment, and that should command the attention of policy makers. Lastly, a commodity can be stored and sold at a later time, but an unemployed person cannot "store" their abilities for resale tomorrow. They generally require employment on an ongoing basis, or at least with some certainty (indeed, with a guarantee), in order to plan for their family's needs. As Harry Hopkins once observed: "People don't eat in the long run, they eat every day."

Better Control of Inflation and Government Spending

As the gold and granary examples show, an employment buffer stock would stabilize the price of a most essential resource in the economy (labor), which is an input of production for any other commodity, thus stabilizing their prices as well. Furthermore, spending on the Job Guarantee program *itself* would offset deflationary pressures (when it expands in recessions) and inflationary pressures (when it shrinks in expansions). Thus, it would be a superior inflation control mechanism than unemployment. No doubt there are other sources of inflation – supply shocks, firm monopoly pricing power, imported inflation – but with a Job Guarantee, government spending on maintaining full employment would not be one of them.

The Job Guarantee would also serve as a superior method for regulating the government's full employment budget. Compare the program to current practice. How many contracts would a government need to provide to firms, and how high a profit should they guarantee to nudge corporations to hire all jobseekers, including the long-term unemployed? What would it take to induce them to raise the wages of their low-wage workers? How many subsidies and how many tax incentives? There is no limit to the budget that would be necessary to coax firms to ensure full employment. Remember, firms are not in the business of hiring every person who seeks work. But with a Job Guarantee, we know the amount of government spending required to maintain full employment – not a dollar more than what would be needed to hire the last person who showed up at the unemployment office. The Job Guarantee by itself would not eliminate no-bid contracts to firms, but by ensuring that they are not the go-to policies for full employment, it would better regulate government spending on job creation. And if price pressures came from other parts of the government's budget policy – e.g., directing spending to industries already operating at capacity – then policy would need to deal with these sources of inflation separately. This is not the place to discuss what a comprehensive agenda for inflation management might look like, but the main message is this: laying off workers is not the answer.

Automatic Stabilizers: Guaranteed Employment or Guaranteed Unemployment?

In the universe of macroeconomic stabilization policies there are *only two* options: either we continue to rely on the existing *unemployment stabilizer* or we replace it with an *employment stabilizer*. The Job Guarantee is the latter – a living-wage employment program that expands and shrinks with changes in economic conditions – and it can be paired with any other program that may be considered desirable for other reasons.

Recently, there has been a resurgence in interest in beefing up automatic stabilizers. There are many. Public policies that deal with some aspect of economic insecurity often have countercyclical features – Medicaid, food and housing assistance, even Social Security – as families increasingly tap these programs when unemployment rises. Without the Job Guarantee, all countercyclical policies (however weak or strong) by necessity continue to use unemployment to soften economic fluctuations. Policy packages that do not include a Job Guarantee need to justify why they require involuntary unemployment (however large or small) as a permanent feature of the economy.

In sum, government guarantees in the form of public options and price support schemes are quite common. By combining the best features of each, the Job Guarantee absolves the policy maker from having to choose between unemployment and inflation. Full employment would be maintained over the long run by providing dignified living-wage job opportunities on standby, while the countercyclical behavior of the program and its robust wage floor would stabilize prices and the economy. The Job Guarantee is the antidote to the NAIRU.

Prevention, Not Just Cure

The Job Guarantee does not just cure unemployment. It has important preventative features as well. First, it frustrates the explosive nature of mass layoffs. Without a Job Guarantee, any policy to tackle unemployment (stimulus, tax cuts, income support) always arrives too little and too late while the avalanche of job losses is well underway. But when the Job Guarantee provides employment opportunities to the newly unemployed on standby, it tempers the human yo-yo effect discussed in Chapter 2. Without a Job Guarantee, mass layoffs are self-reinforcing. Unemployment Insurance (UI) and Temporary Assistance to Needy Families (TANF), for example, help put a floor on collapsing demand, but they do not deal with the psychological effects of uncertain job prospects. Families who count on small and short-lived unemployment benefits cut their spending much more drastically than families who know that a living-wage job option is just around the corner.

The Job Guarantee also prevents people from

slipping unwittingly into long-term unemployment, reducing the resulting individual scarring effects and economic problems. As we also discussed in Chapter 2, the social and economic costs of unemployment are so large that creating jobs as a method of inoculation is a worthwhile goal.

These preventative benefits are especially important to states. During Nixon's New Federalism, through a set of policies that were expanded and accelerated by Reagan, the federal government transferred many of its responsibilities for social programs to states. This devolution was adopted on the pretext of allowing for greater state autonomy and flexibility. But, as we will discuss in the next chapter, it turned out to be excessively burdensome to states, which are not monetarily sovereign and do not have the fiscal power of the federal government to support such programs. Worse, the immediate result was a reduction in benefits with the consolidation of categorical grants into block grants, making it more difficult for states to guarantee access to essential public services. Adding insult to injury, in the 1990s states passed balanced-budget amendments necessitating further program cuts, often precisely when they were most needed – in recessions. On the chopping block were usually programs like meals for the hungry, childcare for low-income earners, and other welfare programs.

With a federally funded Job Guarantee program, states would experience significant budget relief at all times (but especially in downturns), as the program would reduce the demands on states for social expenditures. States would still retain their autonomy in designing, implementing, and administering the program (more on this in the next chapter), but they would not have to rely on race-to-the bottom interstate competition to extend expensive subsidies to firms in exchange for little job creation.

The Labor Standard and the New Social Contract

The Job Guarantee forges a new social contract by establishing a labor standard for good jobs. What good is a job if it pays poverty wages? The task before us is to eliminate both unemployment *and* poverty paying jobs. One of the aims of the Job Guarantee is to rethink what constitutes a dignified labor standard – i.e., the minimum acceptable living pay, benefits, working hours and conditions for any working person – and institute this as a program feature. Another is to put an end to the business practice of paying starvation wages.

The road to establishing a labor standard has been long. When FDR called on Frances Perkins to serve as Labor Secretary, she agreed on the condition that he would support a federal minimum wage, a reduction in the working week, and a revitalized public service employment program (among other groundbreaking pieces of legislation). The 40-hour working week she helped pass was a compromise. A very popular earlier bill for 30 hours was narrowly defeated. The minimum wage also did not extend to all workers. Today, it does not supply a living standard either. The equally popular campaign for $15/hour has made slow legislative progress at the state level, while a full 40 percent of working people in the US earn below that rate. Federal action that extends beyond strengthening labor laws or raising the minimum wage is required.

The Job Guarantee would help secure a true minimum wage for the economy as a whole. As noted, below poverty-wage jobs would face competition from the living-wage public option and firms would be pressured to meet this standard when they hire. Some worry that this feature of the program would attract millions of currently employed low-wage workers from the private sector. But there is little reason to fear such an exodus because firms would necessarily respond to meet the new standard.

Firms regularly match newly mandated wages as a result of local living-wage ordinances, and would do the same in the case of a Job Guarantee. And as Amazon demonstrated recently – largely because it was shamed into raising its wages to $15/hour[5] – they can do so literally overnight.

Second, it is not reasonable to expect that the companies facing wage competition from the Job Guarantee would shut down their stores. Families would continue to eat at fast food restaurants and shop at Walmart or Home Depot. More likely, the new income would create stronger demand and more favorable economic conditions, raising firms' incomes and profits. This would help them match the Job Guarantee wage and increase employment. The research on the minimum wage is clear: wage increases do not cost jobs.[6] Recent research on the Job Guarantee also models these effects (summarized in the next chapter) and finds that, far from creating an exodus, the Job Guarantee permanently increases growth and employment in the private sector.

For southern states with already low minimum wages and higher than average poverty and unemployment rates, the $15/hour Job Guarantee wage could be an effective development strategy by raising incomes, employment, and demand proportionately faster than in states with higher wages and employment. States or cities could still choose to supplement the Job Guarantee minimum wage as they do with living-wage ordinances today.

Finally, the Job Guarantee could help lower the working week standard if it offered full-time pay and benefits for 35-hours of work per week, for example. Germany and France already enjoy a 35-hour working week, and unions in Germany recently got it reduced to 28 hours for millions of workers.[7]

Boon to the Service Sector

This new labor standard would be especially beneficial to service sector workers. The vast majority of workers who would transition to private sector employment from the Job Guarantee would take up service sector jobs, as manufacturing today employs less than 8 percent of the total labor force in the US. The decline in manufacturing employment is a global trend, and even manufacturing giants like China and South Korea cannot count on this sector to maintain previous levels of employment. We often think with nostalgia about manufacturing jobs, longing for the family security they provided and the communities they engendered. But it is easy to forget that manufacturing jobs were precarious and underpaid until organized labor unionized them and governments legislated for workplace safety, working hour limits, and minimum wages. Those changes were far-reaching but still inadequate. They depended on the mutual expectations and obligations between workers and employers over labor conditions. The social contract, which ushered in family wages for men (but only "pin money" for women), is now long gone, and service sector work does not provide comparable wage support and living standards.

Yet the overwhelming majority of jobs in the economy are what we could broadly call *care work*; that is, service sector employment that deals with nurturing and reproducing society. We transport ourselves, feed and clothe ourselves, entertain ourselves, and educate and heal ourselves. But many of these jobs are undervalued and underpaid. How can we do for service jobs what we once did for manufacturing jobs? Minimum wage and work safety laws are not enough.

The Job Guarantee offers a different contract with the American public. Multinational corporations today have no incentive to do what Ford once did – raise worker pay to boost purchasing power and

61

demand for the products the corporation makes. As a structural policy, the living-wage public option for jobs provides the incentive. It puts corporations' feet to the fire and requires that, if they wish to do business in a country that has implemented a Job Guarantee, they must at least match the program's pay.

One may wonder whether corporations would respond by simply outsourcing more jobs to low-wage countries. However, the service sector employs nearly 80 percent of all workers in the US and most service sector jobs cannot be outsourced easily. Call centers and some accounting services maybe, but schools, grocery stores, restaurants, transportation, home repair services, health clinics, dialysis centers, retirement homes, golf courses, and theaters cannot be shipped abroad. Nor are they being radically automated. The primary threat hanging over workers in this sector is not outsourcing or automation, but downsizing, pay cuts, harassment, benefit loss, or other difficult working conditions employers create in the race to cut costs. A worker has no power to say "no" to a bad job unless they are guaranteed the option of a good job with decent pay.

Other Benefits: Transition, Pre-distribution, and the Safety Net

While the Job Guarantee establishes the wage-benefit floor private employers have to meet, it would also serve as a job-placement program. It would allow people to transition from unemployment to employment, and from the Job Guarantee to other private, public, or non-profit work. It would train and prepare them for other employment opportunities via on-the-job training, credentialing, education and other wraparound services. A Job Guarantee could be especially helpful to young people having trouble securing their first job, inmates looking for work, the long-term unemployed with significant barriers to reemployment, and caregivers who may wish to return to the labor market. It could be a stepping-stone to other opportunities. Still, the private sector would not hire everyone, even when every effort has been made to transition as many people as possible out of the public program. The Job Guarantee would continue to provide an ongoing employment safety net for the rest.

The economy-wide living-wage floor would give millions of families a significant pay raise. This would help reduce income inequality, as wages at the bottom would rise faster than those at the top.

The Job Guarantee would use pre-distribution to help tackle inequality by boosting employment and the labor share of income, and by generating more socially useful output. To be sure, it is not a panacea to runaway inequality, and policies to address the increasing concentration of wealth and incomes at the top would also be needed.

The Job Guarantee could help strengthen other aspects of the social safety net. Comprehensive programs like Social Security, for example, still have trouble providing universal coverage. Although only about 4 percent of people would never receive Social Security benefits, 95 percent of them are individuals whose earnings histories are insufficient to qualify them for the program.[8] The poverty rate of infrequent earners on Social Security is 57 percent. The Job Guarantee would provide them with the option of continuous work to qualify for Social Security and the possibility of transitioning to employment opportunities that provide more generous retirement support.

The Job Guarantee could also strengthen education policies and immigration reform. McMillan Cottom has argued that it could be the single best educational reform because it would increase the returns to education for all students and especially students of color,[9] ensuring that desperation no longer shaped working families' choices. With respect to immigration reform, the Job Guarantee could provide employment opportunities to "Dreamers," protected under Deferred Action for Childhood Arrivals (DACA). DACA recipients are allowed to obtain driver's licenses, enroll in college, and legally secure jobs, but the Job Guarantee would ensure that the jobs are readily available. With additional legislation, program participation could be a path to citizenship for Dreamers, parents, and other undocumented immigrants.

The safety net is designed to provide economic security for those who work and for those who do not. The Job Guarantee is a program for working families that complements other forms of income support. People with disabilities, caregivers, students, and the retired all need economic security, and other policies could be passed or existing policies strengthened to address their needs – generous disability and caregiver assistance, universal child allowance, student debt relief, tuition-free public college, and a living retirement income are just a few. Still, the Job Guarantee is designed to improve the lives of non-workers as well. As will be discussed in detail in Chapter 5, the program is organized around *care* and *conservation* work. It prioritizes the kind of public services that benefit children, the elderly, caregivers, and people with disabilities. It offers internships and transitional job opportunities for graduates. It is coupled with universal high-quality early childcare and afterschool activities to alleviate the unpaid care burden of families and the double shift of caregivers who still wish to take up paid work. It can supply meals-on-wheels, companionship, transportation to medical appointments, and other services that could significantly improve the lives of people who do not work. Importantly, surveys show that stay-at-home parents, caregivers, and people with disabilities often want to take paid work for non-financial reasons, but they face significant obstacles to employment. The Job Guarantee provides the missing employment opportunities, along with universal childcare and other needed wraparound services.

The ambition of the Job Guarantee is to transform the macroeconomic stabilization model, provide environmentally sustainable public service employment opportunities on demand, and secure an unapologetic living-wage labor standard for all. As we will discuss in the next chapter, the obstacles to reaching this goal are not financial.

4

But How Will You Pay for It?

"But how will you pay for it?" is the most misleading question in politics today, largely because it is predicated on the myth that the US federal government can run out of funding. In fact, it is no longer even a question. It's an objection, a cordon around many policy proposals. Politicians use it to underfund vital programs in the name of artificial debt limits, unjustified pay-go accounting practices, and painful balanced-budget amendments. And most economists have not helped either. Much like it is with the NAIRU, they have prioritized fictitious debt- and deficit-to-GDP ratios over policies in the public interest.

Cost and budget considerations must rest on the unambiguous understanding that any monetarily sovereign government, like that in the US, may run out of real resources – human or natural – but it cannot run out of finance. Accordingly, answering the question of "how to pay for the Job Guarantee" is much easier than addressing "how to implement it and make it workable" (to be addressed in the next chapter). Here, we tackle the "pay for" question in three ways: 1) by examining the nature of the monetary system and the power of the public purse, 2) by comparing spending on the Job Guarantee to existing unemployment-fighting policies, and 3) by offering specific Job Guarantee budget estimates and criteria for effective financing over the long run.

Monetary Systems and the Power of the Public Purse

There is an important economic reason why large-scale safety nets, public options, price support schemes, and other guarantees are normally the responsibility of the federal government. This is because the buck stops – or more precisely, starts – with the state. Literally.

Every government around the world has the exclusive privilege of issuing and controlling its own currency, even if some nations abdicate this prerogative. The significance of this basic and unde-niable fact is almost universally ignored. It gives a government its monetary sovereignty, its unqualified and flexible spending power to fund its economic affairs. Articulating the nature of monetary sovereignty is at the heart of an economic approach, known as modern monetary theory (MMT), that has attracted global attention.[1] While an exposition of MMT is beyond the scope of this book, its main message is clear enough, and critical: the currency is a simple public monopoly, a creature of government, and a public good that is *already* being issued and spent into existence when the government finances its policy priorities.

The public intuitively understands this. We regularly witness the US government immediately "finding the money" when it finances bank bailouts, billionaire tax cuts, or endless wars. No borrowing from China, no robbing of our unborn grandchildren, no cap-in-hand tax collections from wealthy households are called upon to fund these initiatives. Congress votes for the programs, appropriates the budget, and issues the check, which the Federal Reserve then clears. And no US government checks bounce. Ever.

To put it another way, government spending supplies the economy with currency, while tax payments remove some of it from circulation. The latter has the effect of offsetting any potential inflationary impact of the spending. Taxes also have important distributional and incentive effects but, in a world of fiat and floating sovereign currencies, they do not "pay for" federal government spending, as conventionally understood.

This was clearly articulated by NY Fed chairman Beardsley Ruml in an important 1946 article titled "Taxes for Revenue are Obsolete,"[2] as well as by Fed Chair Ben Bernanke in the aftermath of the Great Financial Crisis. After Congress had appropriated a budget in September 2008 and authorized the Fed to purchase hundreds of billions of dollars of non-performing bank assets, Bernanke clarified: "It's not tax-payer money ... we simply use the computer to mark up the size of the account."[3]

These very same funding powers extend to all spheres of the public purpose. Guaranteeing full employment at stable prices is at the top of the list of public benefits. Indeed, the exclusive privilege to spend its own resource (i.e., the currency) gives the government the exclusive responsibility to do so in a way that ensures economic security for all. The ability of a monetarily sovereign government to guarantee its public options over the long run depends, not on the availability of finance, but on the availability of *real* resources. So long as there are unemployed resources for sale in the domestic currency, the government can always afford to employ them. Paying for the Job Guarantee would mean that the currency put into circulation through the program is always backed by some concrete, socially useful work.

Understanding this changes everything – from the economic possibilities before us to what the public can rightfully demand from its government. Some countries relinquish this fundamental sovereign power (for example when they join monetary unions), and as a consequence surrender a most essential public function – to guarantee certain aspects of the social safety net, from bank deposits, to social insurance, to default risk-free government debt.

The question then is not how to pay for the Job Guarantee, but what the specific economic consequences are of implementing it. It is thus useful to separate the real from the financial costs of the program and compare them to the real and financial costs of continuing with the unemployment status quo. On both counts the Job Guarantee is superior.

Real versus Financial Costs and Benefits

If a monetarily sovereign government is not financially constrained, how then do we evaluate what is money well spent? What criteria shall we use to ensure that public money is effectively employed for the public good?

One criterion would be to consider the relative employment effects of different government job creation policies – the proverbial "bang for the buck" but in terms of net new jobs. Another would be to consider the Job Guarantee's ability to reduce the existing long-term costs of unemployment, both real and financial. A third criterion would be the budget's ability to move anti-cyclically, shrinking in an inflationary environment and expanding in a deflationary environment, while maintaining full employment.

Consider the stabilization efforts undertaken in the aftermath of the Great Financial Crisis. Through the American Recovery and Reinvestment Act of 2009, US Congress appropriated $848 billion to be spent over four years to resuscitate the economy. By official estimates, this stimulus created or *saved* on average between 1.3 and 4.7 million jobs per year from 2009 to 2012[4] – a dismal result when official unemployment during that time averaged between 12.5 and 15 million people per year (and using the expanded definition, peaked at 30 million).[5] The $848 billion budget was quite conventional – it prioritized tax cuts, extended unemployment insurance and other income support, and offered subsidies and contracts to firms. Had there been a Job Guarantee program in place, the budget would have been sufficient to create 20 million living-wage jobs (including a generous allowance for materials and benefits),[6] wiping out the entire official and some of the hidden unemployment. It is more than likely that the government would not have ended up employing all 20 million people. Had it gotten the ball rolling and started hiring the unemployed directly, it would have halted the avalanche of lay-offs. (Remember that in early 2009, the economy was losing on average 750,000 jobs per month.) It would have launched a job-led recovery, encouraging firms to resume their own hiring. This direct employment approach would have averted the most protracted jobless recovery in postwar history.

Could the government have funded a larger stimulus in 2009? No doubt. Would a doubling or tripling of the recovery package have helped speed up the recovery? Surely. Would a larger government deficit have created a job for everyone who wanted one? Unlikely. As we discussed in Chapter 3, there are many reasons why firms do not hire all of the unemployed even in good times, and there is no limit to the amount of government spending that would be required to persuade them to do so in the depths of a recession. The Job Guarantee, by contrast, ensures that every person who shows up at the unemployment office is hired. It provides stronger countercyclical stabilization for a relatively smaller full employment budget (i.e., spending per job created) than the conventional stimulus approach, and a firmer cap on government spending for the purposes of securing full employment.

Tax cuts and subsidies are widely used in normal times as well. Federal subsidies to industries are in the hundreds of billions of dollars. Some support prices and profits (e.g., in the agricultural or financial sectors), others promote the private provisioning of essential public goods (e.g., in healthcare or education), but many are given with the explicit intent to stimulate employment. As a job-creation tool, subsidies are especially problematic for states, which are not monetarily sovereign like the federal government. Cross-border subsidy competition among states deprives them of needed tax revenue, whereas the job creation effect is small. Studies show that these state and municipal tax subsidies primarily shift jobs from one state to another.[7] A federally funded Job Guarantee not only produces the highest primary, secondary, and induced employment effects, it also frees states from engaging in an arms race to retain businesses and attract firms from other states.

But How Will You Pay for It?

As Chapter 2 documented, unemployment is expensive and already paid for. Its large social and economic costs compound and multiply the longer we tolerate it. Any spending on the Job Guarantee would be both an investment in our human and natural resources and a form of inoculation against the major social costs of unemployment. Consider mass incarceration in the US. The average annual cost per inmate in 2015 was over $33,000. That is the equivalent of one living-wage job with benefits per adult for a household with two working adults and two children.[8] In many states the cost per inmate is much higher, sometimes twice the national average. At the same time, the barriers to employment for individuals with a criminal record are very high, while the link between unemployment and recidivism is well established. Total public spending on incarceration has been soaring without reducing recidivism. Yet jobs programs for former inmates have proven to drastically reduce rates of reoffending. Simultaneously, dismally paid prison labor is used to perform essential public functions (e.g., California pays inmates $2/day and $1/hour to fight its raging wildfires), displacing regular public sector employees.[9]

This is but one example of the direct financial and real costs of unemployment. In virtually all corners of the economy one can find examples of the government allocating significant resources to deal with socioeconomic and environmental adversities (homelessness, poverty, floods, pollution), instead of focusing on common-sense prevention and rehabilitation (building homes, providing jobs, fortifying the infrastructure). The power of the public purse prescribes that the fiscally responsible approach would be to "pay" for employment and renewal instead of neglect and privation.

The Job Guarantee Budget

Estimates of the direct government expenditures on the Job Guarantee would depend on the state of the economy. Because private sector employment moves cyclically, the Job Guarantee will necessarily move countercyclically. (As the next chapter discusses, real-world examples show such countercyclical features.) Therefore, its budget must be designed to accommodate such fluctuations.

To estimate the budget for the program and put some numbers on its impact on the economy, a research team at the Levy Economics Institute simulated a very ambitious program for the United States with the following characteristics:[10]

- The Job Guarantee wage is $15/hour
- Non-labor costs (materials purchased from the private sector) are 25 percent above labor costs
- Benefits (healthcare, childcare, and paid leave) are an additional 20 percent of the wage bill
- Workers in the program work an average of 32 hours per week, choosing between full- and part-time opportunities
- Job Guarantee workers pay the employee's portion of payroll taxes
- A third of all income generated by the Job Guarantee is subject to federal income taxes
- No additional taxes are levied to offset program costs

The Job Guarantee is simulated using the well-established and stock-flow consistent Fair model for the US. The program is implemented at the start of 2018 and fully phased in over twelve months. The simulation evaluates its impact on growth, private sector employment, poverty, state budgets, and inflation over a ten-year period. It also estimates the program's gross expenditures and net budgetary impact.

Table 2 provides summary statistics for the low- and high-bound scenarios, both of which make conservative assumptions about the amount of

Table 2 Simulating the Job Guarantee

	Low Bound	High Bound
Peak Job Guarantee employment	11.6 million (2022)	15.4 million (2022)
Average Job Guarantee employment thereafter	11.1 million	14.7 million
Peak yearly contribution to real GDP ($2017)	$472 billion (2022)	$593 billion (2022)
Average contribution to real GDP thereafter	$440 billion	$543 billion
Peak increase in private sector employment	3.3 million (2023)	4.2 million (2023)
Average increase in private employment thereafter	2.93 million	3.65 million
Increase in inflation	peak 0.63 percent (2020) declining to 0.11 percent	peak 0.74 percent (2020) declining to 0.09 percent
Improvement in state budgets	$35 billion	$55 billion
Average direct spending on the Job Guarantee	$409 billion (2020–27)	$543 billion (2020–27)
Average net budgetary impact	$247.5 billion	$340 billion
Net budgetary impact as percent of GDP	0.98 percent of GDP	1.33 percent of GDP

Source: L. Randall Wray et al., "Public Service Employment: A Path to Full Employment," Levy Institute Research Project Report, Annandale-on-Hudson, NY: Levy Economics Institute of Bard College, 2018.

tax receipts to be generated from the program and the expected savings on Medicaid and the Earned Income Tax Credit. The model does not account for any additional government savings on anti-poverty programs. The intent is to simulate the budgetary costs and economic effects of a very large and ambitious Job Guarantee program.

With conservative assumptions about the potential savings, the budgetary impact of the program in the higher bound scenario is less than 1.5 percent of GDP per year. It is plausible that if we accounted for all reductions in government sector spending on unemployment, along with all of the positive social and economic multipliers, the program's budget impact would be neutral, though this would not be a criterion for success since in deep downturns the government would normally need to increase its deficit spending.

Additionally, we find that one full-time Job Guarantee worker per family would lift a family of five and 9.5 million children out of poverty (or about 63 percent of all poor children in the US). With one full-time and one part-time Job Guarantee worker per family, the program would lift a family of eight and 12.4 million children out of poverty (or approximately 83 percent of all poor children).

Considering the robust macroeconomic effects and modest reductions in existing costs, the estimated Job Guarantee budget is surprisingly small. In simulation, this large program employs at its peak between 11.6 and 15.4 million people, raises wages for the entire economy (including private firms) to $15/hour, provides generous benefits, and allocates 25 percent of its expenditures to non-labor costs. As a consequence, it boosts real GDP by nearly half a trillion dollars and increases private sector employment by 3 to 4 million jobs without generating any inflationary effect of macroeconomic significance – all for a net budgetary effect of about 1 to 1.3 percent of GDP. This is money well spent.

Federal governments provide public options, price supports, and other public guarantees, not only because they have been charged with the welfare of their citizens, but also because they hold the exclusive power of the public purse. Only a monetarily sovereign government can ensure the ongoing funding for the public options on which its citizens depend. Currently we use the power of the public purse to finance an unemployment regime – a rather dysfunctional and fiscally irresponsible way of using that power. The Job Guarantee proposes that we use our monetary sovereignty to finance an employment regime.

5

What, Where, and How: Jobs, Design, and Implementation

In the midst of the Great Depression, the New Deal launched employment projects in every single county in the United States within a few short months. Today, these counties have unemployment offices, making up a network of American Job Centers. This network is coordinated by the Department of Labor and provides the full range of support services to jobseekers under one roof, except one – the assurance of a decent job. The proposal in this book is to convert these unemployment offices into genuine employment offices, as discussed in Chapter 1.

What would it take to do so? How could we ensure that there are enough jobs for all jobseekers? What exactly would they do? How would the program be organized and managed?

As we answer these questions, we hope to demonstrate that: 1) there are many existing projects and

81

initiatives that could be scaled up for the purposes of implementing the Job Guarantee in a decentralized manner; 2) it is not necessary to reinvent the wheel as we could draw on best practices from the past and from around the world; 3) there are many urgent, ongoing, and nice-to-have projects that could create millions of jobs for decades to come; and 4) the program holds significant democratizing potential.

Program Features

To deliver the countercyclical, structural, and preventative benefits described earlier, the Job Guarantee proposal suggests the following design features. The program is *voluntary* and *inclusive*. It is open to anyone of legal working age who wants to work, irrespective of labor market status, race, sex, color, or creed. It is not a replacement for traditional public works or essential government services. It is not charity or a subsidy (people are paid to work), neither is it a means-tested workfare policy threatening to remove a person's benefits unless they show up for work. It does, however, reduce welfare expenditures that are no longer necessary due to the living-income floor the Job Guarantee has provided.

The program is also *permanent* and *targeted*, in order to serve as an automatic stabilizer and tackle cyclical and structural unemployment. The *base wage-benefit package is fixed* to establish a price anchor and a firm floor to all wages. The proposed wage is $15 per hour to hasten the national push for doubling the federal minimum wage. Because $15 may well not be enough to maintain living standards in just a few years, the program would have a statutory wage/benefit review every few years to adjust the figure as needed. Benefits include Social Security, health insurance and professionalized childcare, and paid leave (as the US is the only major country without such leave).

The program is *federally funded* but *locally administered* in a decentralized manner. It is managed by states, municipalities, non-profits, social enterprises, and cooperatives, which conduct assessments of local needs and design projects to meet them (more on this below). The American Job Centers would act as *community jobs banks* that solicit project proposals from local organizations. These are the proverbial on-the-shelf jobs that are designed with care, though some experimentation would be needed and welcome.

With the exception of some youth apprenticeship projects, the Job Guarantee would not normally create jobs in the private sector. The focus is on *public service employment*, so as not to compete with private sector activities and to help tackle the twin problems of "poverty in the midst of plenty" and "public squalor in the midst of private opulence." It is not a stretch to imagine many employment projects, as suggested in Chapter 1, that could be staffed with people who have different abilities and experience (more examples are provided below).

Only the public sector can offer an employment guarantee. It is neither possible nor desirable to oblige firms to do so. Firm hiring is pro-cyclical, while the Job Guarantee is countercyclical. Also the private sector does not create jobs that fit the skills and needs of jobseekers. There, hiring works the other way around – workers are fitted to private firms' job needs. The Job Guarantee creates more vacancies than jobseekers, thus *matching* employment opportunities to people's abilities.

The Job Guarantee provides *training*, education, credentialing, and apprenticeship opportunities to allow people to *transition* out of the program into other forms of paid work. It is sensitive to the specific needs of veterans, at-risk youths, former inmates, and people with disabilities. It prioritizes *care jobs* that address all forms of neglect – whether of people in need, communities in disrepair, or an environment in peril.

The Job Guarantee proposal approaches unemployment as a public health concern, not only because of the way it affects family and community health, but also because of the way it spreads. The contagion effect of mass layoffs from one area to another and from epicenter to periphery suggests that unemployment spreads like a virus and should be treated as such. Thus, the Job Guarantee is designed around the concepts of *preparedness* and *prevention*. When it comes to epidemics, the national crisis response aims not to wait until the last minute. We plan. We prepare. We prevent. Consider how the Strategic National Stockpile – the nation's largest repository of essential pharmaceuticals and medical supplies – responds to public health threats. The government maintains warehouses throughout the country that can distribute vaccines, medication, and other supplies to local areas in the event of an emergency. In a similar way, the American Job Centers will solicit projects from participating local organizations on an ongoing basis to ensure that there are enough shelved projects able to provide jobs on demand.

With respect to the *budget*, the main criterion is that it is flexible and *fluctuates countercyclically*. There are several ways to do this. One is to fund the program out of the general budget, as we do with Medicare Part D, making it permanently solvent without artificial constraints like trust funds. Another is to use a combination of base and supplemental appropriations, as we do with disaster and emergency relief. Payments for program wages and materials can be disbursed to state and local Department of Labor offices, the same way we disburse emergency unemployment insurance benefits.

Administration and Participatory Democracy

While the buck stops with the Department of Labor, which must ultimately ensure that the Job Guarantee mandate is met, the program is better administered in a decentralized manner. Municipalities in cooperation with community groups could conduct assessment surveys, cataloguing community needs and available resources as they design the community jobs banks. Community organizations, non-profits, social entrepreneurial ventures, and cooperatives can also apply for funds directly to the Department of Labor. Grants are approved contingent on 1) creation of employment opportunities for unemployed people; 2) no displacement effect of existing workers; and 3) useful activities performed, measured by their social and environmental impact.

The Job Guarantee need not reinvent the wheel in terms of administrative infrastructure, as a fair amount of it already exists. The American Job Centers already provide payments (unemployment insurance) to the unemployed, job search assistance, referrals, training, GED completion, résumé building, English as a second language lessons, math and reading training, and other one-on-one services, such as stress and financial management courses. At the same time, localities, municipalities, and non-profits already run projects that address public needs. All of them are understaffed and underfunded. The Job Guarantee will build on the existing administrative and institutional framework to match needs with resources.

Applied globally, the administration of the program will be country specific. For example, in Argentina, a very decentralized network of community groups had designed and managed its projects, while in Brussels a sophisticated infrastructure of employment and training options, caseworkers, and comprehensive wraparound services are provided to the unemployed by one public agency (more on this below).

The goal is to offer a rewarding activity that ensures social recognition and empowers participants via a *bottom-up design*, encouraging direct input from citizens, community members, and other stakeholders representing the public interest in the proposal, management, and execution of the projects. Such a *participatory democracy* approach can be found in many places around the world, from the zero-unemployment-zone experiments in France to democratically run public works projects in Brazil and Germany. Participatory budgeting models globally use citizen assemblies, information technology, and different organizational methods to ensure citizen input on local projects and budgeting allocation. Endorsed by international organizations such as the UN and the World Bank, participatory and gender-aware budgeting significantly improves effectiveness, equity, and the overall results of such programs.

Because the Job Guarantee program encourages citizen input, puts pressure on punitive private sector labor practices, and invests in the public good, it can be an institution with profound democratizing tendencies, functioning as a conduit for transformative change in the workplace, in people's everyday lives, and in the economy as a whole.

Differences from Other Proposals

Before digging into the types of jobs that the program could create, it is helpful to highlight some features that are specific to this proposal. The aspect that unites all Job Guarantees is the human rights framework and the focus on jobs with dignity and a minimum standard.[1] The differences tend to center around the level and structure of the Job Guarantee wage and the program's administration and management.

The proposal presented here favors a fixed living wage with basic benefits, as opposed to tiered wages.[2] A tiered wage structure caused much political wrangling during the New Deal era and ultimately undermined support for many projects. A tiered structure also does not have the price stabilization features described earlier. The program's minimum wage floor pressures private employers to match it, but it does not compete with them for skilled workers *across* the wage spectrum, which can cause wage bidding for skilled workers who already enjoy comparatively stronger income growth and better employment conditions. The goal here is to firmly secure the living-wage floor.

The Job Guarantee wage in this proposal is also not indexed to inflation, so as not to embed an automatic wage-price inflationary mechanism. Instead it incorporates legislation for regular reviews and mandatory increases of the wage, in lockstep with increases in productivity, to ensure it maintains a decent living standard. Note that, since the Job Guarantee would more than double the current minimum wage (from $7.25 to $15/hour), it could produce a one-time jump in prices as firms adjust to the new higher wage level. However, this one-time increase should not be confused with inflation – which is a continuous increase in the price level. Such a significant one-time wage increase would not be unprecedented. In 1949, the minimum wage was nearly doubled without accelerating inflation, at a time when the economy was as close to true full employment as it has ever been in the postwar era.

Additionally, this proposal favors a highly decentralized administration. Job Guarantee workers are not typically federal employees even though the program is federally funded. The decentralized model is preferred for several reasons. First, depending on the state of the economy, the program may need to employ as much as 10 percent of the labor force. This would require expanding the federal labor force fivefold. States, localities, and non-profits are much better suited to accommodate such an expansion by comparison, as they already comprise about 20 percent of total employment.

Including non-religious and non-political non-profit organizations into the program's administration would have a significant democratizing potential. Such organizations are an important source of social innovation and the federal government already contracts with them. A plurality of local non-profits and cooperatives can enhance democratic decision making. Local advocacy groups already put pressure on the federal government to help address their constituents' concerns, and cooperatives have been shown to empower their members, increase asset creation, and reinvest in their communities. Indeed, the public purpose is already met by a broad set of intertwined institutions. Engaging them in the Job Guarantee design could help broaden civil society.

The present proposal also does not rely on large-scale infrastructure for job creation. Infrastructure investment is a permanent function of government that has been grossly underfunded and neglected. Vital levee, bridge, and highway projects should not fluctuate with the business cycle, nor should they be discontinued in expansions. And as they are often staffed with high-skilled union workers, the Job Guarantee must take great care not displace them. But the Job Guarantee can organize smaller projects that can be added or postponed, depending on economic conditions. It can also unionize its own workforce. Putting in place and fortifying our nation's infrastructure to prevent, mitigate, and withstand the impact of intensifying hurricanes, tornadoes, fires, and floods requires immediate action and a large labor force. If a major infrastructure program were attempted as part of the Green New Deal industrial policy, the Job Guarantee itself would be much smaller than in its absence.

Types of Jobs: A "National Care Act"

One thousand women on horseback. These were the roving New Deal librarians who, starting in 1935, brought books and set up libraries in the most remote areas of Kentucky. The women rode across twenty-nine counties, sometimes over 100 miles a day. And where the terrain was difficult, they dismounted their horses and carried the books on foot. Their impact was far-reaching. As one recipient put it: "Them books you brought us has saved our lives."[3] The Works Progress Administration (WPA) library projects, which served forty-five states and employed 14,500 people, helped solve two problems at once – unemployment and illiteracy. These "unskilled" unemployed women provided a public library option to the most remote regions in the nation at a time when most libraries were primarily privately funded and most people had no access to books. They supported a public initiative for something we consider today to be a permanent fixture of social life – public libraries in every corner of the country.

Today, our communities have entirely different needs and a much greater capacity for solving them. Horse-riding librarians are no longer needed, but there is a different kind of neglect communities suffer stemming from environmental factors and the underfunding of essential public services. Once we broaden our understanding of productive work, the sky is the limit for organizing projects. For example, programs to address the looming environmental challenges can create millions of public service jobs for years to come. And while there is endless invisible environmental work that can be done by people with different skills, there is also a lot of important care work that is undervalued, underpaid, and altogether ignored. Green jobs are defined here as those that address all forms of destitution and neglect of our most valuable resources, both natural and human. Thus the Job Guarantee is conceived as a national care plan that prioritizes care for the environment, care for the people, and care for the community.

Care for the Environment

In the 1930s, FDR's Tree Army planted 3 billion trees, created and rehabilitated 711 state parks, built 125,000 miles of truck trails, developed 800 new state parks, controlled soil erosion on 40 million acres of farm land, improved grazing conditions on public domain ranges, and increased the wildlife population.[4] These projects breathed a new life into the US conservation movement, the forerunner of today's climate activism.

While unemployment and the Dust Bowl presented an existential threat to many rural communities during the Great Depression, the climate crisis today is of planetary proportions. Many of the most acute environmental problems occur precisely where people live – in urban and rural settings. The infrastructure is overwhelmed by water runoff, cities are threatened by forest fires, and residential communities are nesting beside hazardous waste sites. Cities are already thinking of urban tree planting as public health infrastructure that can keep air clean and cool, regulate temperatures, and support water quality and runoff. The environmental projects one could conceive of are endless – flood control, environmental surveys, species monitoring, tree planting, park maintenance and renewal, removal of invasive plants, building local fisheries. Projects can create community and rooftop gardens, strengthen fire and disaster prevention measures, weatherize homes, or launch composting and sustainable agriculture initiatives to address the food-desert problem in the US.

Care for the Community

Rebuilding the environment also means rebuilding communities. Jobs could include cleanup of vacant properties, reclaiming materials, restoration and other small infrastructure projects, setting up school gardens, urban farms, co-working spaces, solar arrays, tool libraries, and classes and programs, as well as building playgrounds, restoring historical sights, organizing community theaters, car-pooling programs, recycling, reuse and water collection initiatives, food waste programs, and oral histories projects.

Care for the People

The issues facing the people who live in those communities extend beyond the above-mentioned environmental challenges. Provision of elderly care, afterschool activities, meals-on-wheels, and special programs for children, at-risk youths, veterans, former inmates, and people with disabilities can all be part of the Job Guarantee program. Since the program provides job opportunities to the very people benefitting from these programs, it also gives them agency. For example, veterans or people with disabilities can help run the very outreach programs they count on for support.

Other examples could include organizing nutrition surveys in schools, health awareness programs for young mothers, adult skills classes in schools and local libraries, or extended day programs, as well as shadowing teachers, coaches, hospice workers, and librarians. The Job Guarantee could also organize urban campuses, co-ops, classes and training, and apprenticeships in sustainable agriculture.

All of the above-mentioned community care jobs could produce a new generation of urban teachers, artists and artisans, makers, and inventors. In fact, all of these tasks are already being done in one form or another. But all of them are in short supply, lacking enough helping hands and a budget to employ them. The Job Guarantee can fill this gap and scale up already existing best practices and projects.

Real World Programs

There is also much that can be learnt from direct employment programs around the world. These are often well targeted but temporary. A notable exception is India's National Rural Employment Guarantee Act (NREGA), which (although it is not universal) enshrines the right to employment into law, guaranteeing at least 100 days of paid work to each rural household per year. Examples of other large-scale programs past and present include the US New Deal, Argentina's Plan Jefes, South Africa's Expanded Public Works Program, and the Swedish corporatist postwar model, where the government effectively acted as an employer of last resort up until the late 1980s.

During the 1930s, the New Deal pioneered large-scale public service employment when the unemployment rate in the US approached 30 percent. An estimated 13 million workers participated in the Works Progress Administration – the largest of the jobs programs, which can be credited with bringing the United States into the twentieth century.[5] It created jobs, set up a wide range of public service initiatives, and built the infrastructure that supported the war effort and the postwar boom. Similarly, Argentina's Plan Jefes was launched in

97

2001 when unemployment rates exceeded 20 percent, but it focused primarily on smaller community programs. The New Deal and Plan Jefes demonstrated that a centralized program (the former) and a decentralized one (the latter) can be up and running on short order.

Both programs had clear countercyclical behavior. Unemployment began to decline as a result of the New Deal in the depths of the Great Depression, but spiked again during the Roosevelt recession, when FDR briefly reversed course and tried to balance the budget. Argentina's program ballooned soon after implementation (hiring 13 percent of the labor force) and declined steadily as the economy recovered and workers transitioned to private sector employment.[6] Plan Jefes had a significant positive impact on workers and their families, and especially on women.

Today, India's NREGA program is credited with creating many productive public assets in rural communities (wells, ponds, roads, parks) and providing needed public services such as water conservation, horticulture, flood prevention, drought proofing, and other environmental projects. The program has reduced the pay gap between men and women amongst the poor, and has helped raise wages at the bottom for private sector workers.[7]

Smaller jobs programs also offer useful insights, such as the very successful Youth Job Guarantee in Brussels, which is being expanded to all unemployed people, and the zero long-term unemployment regions in France. In the US, the Youth Incentive Entitlement Pilot Projects (YIEPP), which ran from 1978 to 1980, guaranteed employment to 76,000 youths. In its short life, it sharply reduced youth unemployment in the areas where it was implemented, closing the employment-to-population gap between black and white youths, and helping participants transition to private sector employment opportunities within thirteen months (even though the guarantee was for two years). Similarly, the 2009 Future Jobs Fund in the UK managed to transition 43 percent of its participants into permanent employment within a year (before it was reformed into a punitive workfare program). The UK's National Institute of Economic and Social Research called it one of the most successful programs in recent history, and found that it 1) enhanced public service work, 2) was well targeted to the most disadvantaged youth groups – the long-term unemployed, 3) improved their specialized and transferrable skills and employability, and 4) reduced their time on welfare.[8]

Today, small direct job creation programs are

scattered around the United States. In Albuquerque, the city government gives jobs to homeless people, successfully connecting them to permanent employment and housing, inspiring other municipalities to do the same.[9] Various programs that place ex-convicts into jobs boast significant reductions in recidivism rates.[10] There are also urban programs for at-risk youths and the unemployed, who work in farm lots, cottage businesses, co-working spaces, greenhouses, solar arrays, tool libraries, aquaponics, community gardens, taking classes and organizing afterschool activities and other projects. These are just a few examples of the kinds of projects that can be fostered and expanded, giving an idea of what the Job Guarantee in the United States might look like.

Concerns and Frequently Asked Questions

We have thus far dispensed with the assumption that unemployment is "necessary" to stabilize the economy. But the idea that the federal government should be responsible for job creation always invokes some immediate worries. In particular, that the Job Guarantee would 1) mean a "big-government takeover," 2) be impossible to manage, 3) reduce productivity, 4) create make-work projects, and 5) be dangerously disruptive to the point of stoking a political revolution. Additional issues concern 6) the impact of technology on jobs in general (isn't technology making all jobs obsolete?), 7) the program's countercyclical features (is it even possible to add and shed workers on short notice, and, even if it is, shouldn't socially useful projects be staffed on a permanent basis?), and 8) the political obstacles the program would face (wouldn't politicians and firms ensure that it just won't happen?). We will address each of these concerns in turn.

On Big Government

The worry about big government has it backwards. We already have "big government," devoting hundreds of billions of dollars, time, resources, and administrative effort to dealing with the economic and social costs of unemployment, underemployment, and poverty. As noted, unemployment is already paid for, possibly many times over. The Job Guarantee would *reduce* these federal government costs, while also cutting costs to households, firms, and states.

Far from being a big-government takeover, the size of the Job Guarantee largely depends on the private sector. How many jobs are private firms creating? Are they hiring or automating and outsourcing? How many mass layoffs are in the pipeline? The Job Guarantee responds to changes in the private sector, acting as an economic stabilizer and providing an economic cushion to families.

On Administration

Just as we do not think that there is an optimal level of illiteracy, we do not think that public education must be scrapped because it is an "administrative nightmare." And yet the managerial challenges associated with running a Job Guarantee program are often used as a litmus test of its desirability. Apart from the unique double standard applied to the Job Guarantee (one rarely hears such objections to "nation building" or financial bailouts), it is hardly evident that running it would be an impossibly difficult task. Indeed, history suggests otherwise.

Today, public schools in the US guarantee primary and secondary education to nearly 51 million students. Medicare, Medicaid and CHIP serve 74 million people, and Social Security covers 54 million. Total spending on these programs is approximately 14 percent of GDP. By comparison, the Job Guarantee program aims to employ 11–15 million people to the tune of 1–1.5 percent of GDP.

And while it does no one any good to deny that there will be administrative hurdles specific to the program, they seem no more formidable than those of other policy priorities. The proposal outlined here aims to alleviate them by using as much of the existing institutional infrastructure as possible and facilitating a process of bottom-up job creation.

On Productivity

The claim that the Job Guarantee would be unproductive is also upside-down. Employing someone is *not less* productive than keeping them unemployed. Given the deleterious effects of joblessness on individual and family wellbeing, one could argue that the productivity of the unemployed is actually negative, while the Job Guarantee provides on-the-job training and education. Individuals who enjoy relative job security are happier, more dependable, and all around more productive in the workplace. Green projects rehabilitate the environment, strengthen communities, and improve the social determinants of health. Care jobs (for the young and elderly), along with jobs for artists and musicians, are incorrectly considered unproductive by the narrowest of measures, yet they too increase productivity by enhancing overall welfare and quality of life.

On Make-Work and False Choices

The fear that Job Guarantee projects would necessarily be make-work amounts to what James Galbraith called "an admission of impotence and a call for preemptive surrender."[11] Indeed, New Deal projects were often derided as boondoggles, yet they rebuilt communities, the economy, and people's lives.

The "make-work" canard, however, is not entirely ideological. A charitable interpretation is that it stems from a confusion over purpose. Is the Job Guarantee a program that provides jobs to *everyone* who needs one, or is it a program that creates "productive" projects? If it is a policy for useful work, the argument goes, it cannot possibly employ everyone. If it is a policy for the unemployed, then it cannot possibly be productive.

These of course are false choices. The program is productive *because* it eliminates the negative return from joblessness, and *because* it stabilizes the economy better than unemployment. However, jobs programs that fail to reaffirm the access to a basic job as a human right will inevitably fail to answer the questions that troubled the New Deal projects: Who should be employed? Are they skilled enough? Are the projects useful? Shouldn't they be staffed with more skilled workers? When the emphasis is on the project, rather than on the person, it invariably becomes difficult to advocate for jobs for all. That becomes possible when the emphasis is on the scourge of unemployment and the need to guarantee the basic economic right to a job.

On the Program's "Disruptive" Effects

In the IT world, disruptions are hailed as progressive and innovative. One innovation of the Job Guarantee program is that it compels firms to match its living-wage floor (though this goal would be reached faster if the federal minimum wage were also increased as the program was being implemented). For some critics, this is dangerous because workers outside the program would realize that they do not enjoy the decent pay, healthcare, and childcare of Job Guarantee workers and might stage a "political rebellion."[12] This critique is a thinly veiled argument in support of the firms' privilege to pay poverty wages.

A similar critique plagued the New Deal's Civil Works Administration. As Philip Harvey notes, the problem with the CWA was not that it was unpopular but that it was *widely* popular.[13] Firms (not their workers) protested that the program offered too much job security, and southern racist employers argued that the higher public wages were "ruining"

black workers, giving them the "wrong incentives."
Farmers complained that they were losing cheap
farm workers to the more stable civil public works,
even though the CWA wages were well below the
national average. The political attack came under
the usual pretext that the program was busting the
federal budget and that it was time to cancel it and
replace it with the dole. Had Roosevelt reauthor-
ized the program, it may have been impossible to
ever end it. This was the verdict of FDR's conservative budget director, Lewis Douglas, who was no
friend of the CWA.[14] Workers liked the program
and started to regard the projects it offered as their
right, as something the government owed them.

It is true that one major goal of the Job Guarantee
is to disrupt those businesses that can only be successful by paying poverty wages. Euthanizing
poverty paying jobs through the Job Guarantee is
a feature, not a bug of the program, and the com-
plaints will come from firms not their workers. Even
in the midst of the Great Depression, firms wanted
to keep the threat of the sack, and much preferred a
welfare system that subsidized their access to cheap
labor. But there is no reason to believe that the Job
Guarantee will be violently disruptive to the private
sector. As discussed above, our model indicates that
it significantly increases real GDP and private sector

employment. In reality, although firms protest all increases in the minimum wage, they have no trouble matching them, and the economic benefits of raising wages are well documented.[15]

Critics also want us to fear the impact the Job Guarantee will have on public employment. The worry is that the program's living-wage floor would induce both the private and public sectors to engage in race-to-the bottom wage cutting to match the guaranteed floor. This critique implies that instituting a public option – any public option – degrades the existing benefits of people who may not need to access it. It is like saying that Social Security should not have been implemented because it would have reduced both government and private pensions. But in the US, even federal employees who have Social Security enjoy supplemental federal public retirement plans. Public options do not create a race to the bottom; they raise and secure the floor.

On Technology

Anxieties around technological change are understandable, but it is important to distinguish between two separate questions: "Will technology automate a lot of existing jobs?" (yes they will) and "Will technology cause a 'jobs apocalypse'?" (hardly inevitable).[16] Indeed, as technology changes our lives, the vast majority of jobs of the future have not even been invented yet. And yet, the most dangerous jobs today are not being automated quickly enough (e.g., trucking, meat processing, or electric power line installation). Many of the perilous jobs that also pillage the earth need to be made obsolete altogether, not automated (e.g., onshore and offshore drilling). There is no "iron law of technology" that makes the elimination of certain jobs obligatory. Society chooses how to adopt technology. Despite innumerable online courses, we still pay a premium for high-quality, in-person instruction. Apps, smart boards, and other programs have transformed school curricula, but not the focus on personal contact and interactive learning. Hospice care is not done through a television set and personal care is still the norm.

Despite the glum resignation tech change seems to invite, technology is not the enemy. Jobs are disappearing not because the robots are marching in, but because management, in pursuit of aggressive cost cutting, has pitted workers against machines. Indeed, given the looming environmental problems, technology will be a critical factor in solving them and solving them fast. Does that mean that we cannot find useful things for humans to do? Not at all. Is there a limit to the many ways in which we can serve each other and our communities? Probably not. This is why this Job Guarantee proposal is conceived as a National Care Act. Technological change notwithstanding, we can create many jobs for people that are socially useful. And technology can be embraced as a way of improving our standard of living, not as a force that threatens it.

On the Practicality of Cyclical Employment

Critics also worry that the Job Guarantee cannot function as an effective automatic stabilizer. Can we really create jobs on demand? If they are so useful, why let Job Guarantee workers go when the economy recovers?

This criticism fails to recognize that the private sector behaves cyclically *already*. The ability to absorb or shed employees is not a unique challenge for the Job Guarantee. Indeed every labor market segment within the private, non-profit, or public sectors deals with new entrants and job leavers on an ongoing basis. It is in the nature of the structural and cyclical changes of the economy. But because the Job Guarantee is a better stabilizer than unemployment, it would significantly reduce the current yo-yo effect in labor markets. Smaller fluctuations in private employment mean smaller fluctuations in the Job Guarantee and easier transitions, removing the challenge of accommodating large swaths of people on short notice. Additionally, once the program has been established, many of the specific projects described above could be scaled up or down relatively quickly, as workers enter or leave the Job Guarantee.

Essential and ongoing public services need to be staffed on a permanent basis. The Environmental Protection Agency and the Food and Drug Administration are in need of many more inspectors, but these are not temporary Job Guarantee jobs. Similarly, with respect to the professionalized childcare benefit of the program, it should be noted that this too would be a mainline government function, although these childcare centers could hire temporary trainees and teacher assistants through the program. Professionalized affordable childcare is permanent infrastructure. It is a public option for childcare. Whether working parents have jobs in the Job Guarantee program or elsewhere, they would still need childcare.

On Power and Political Challenges

For several decades, surveys have polled whether the government should guarantee jobs to the unemployed and the results have shown consistent majority support – over 60 percent and more recently as high as 78 percent (see next chapter for details). These figures show that the program bridges the ideological divide and resonates with voters across the political spectrum. Yet policy makers have not been paying attention. Until now. In the US, several 2020 presidential hopefuls have endorsed the Job Guarantee, and dozens of candidates for office at the local and national level have adopted it in their platforms. It was also included as a signature program in the Green New Deal resolution.[17] There has been a groundswell of support for it from many corners of civil society.[18] The moment is ripe for change, and the electorate, especially young voters, are looking for bold solutions to entrenched economic and environmental problems.

The opposition from vested interests should not be underestimated. Yes, Michael Kalecki warned that captains of industry would oppose full employment vigorously.[19] But they opposed the minimum wage too, and the reduction of the working week, and the creation of Social Security, and banning child labor, and allowing women to control their property and earnings, and on and on. Securing the Job Guarantee is another step in the long process of securing economic rights for all.

In some ways, we understand the nature of the opposition and the obstacles better today than in the past. First, implementing employment programs as emergency measures in downturns ensures their rapid expiration date. Second, without the legal right to employment, even quasi-full employment regimes (Sweden, Japan) could not survive the Reagan-Thatcher revolution. Third, the existence of a legal right would not mean that programs would be void of problems, but it would provide the institutional basis for securing the mandate over the long run, even under a neoliberal regime. Some local governments in India, for example, are extending the popular rural employment program to young people in urban areas, and farmers and workers are demanding a nationwide extension to all urban unemployed persons. In the US, the electorate is engaged in a post-Reagan-era rehabilitation of government and the public purpose, opening a window of opportunity to finally secure this fundamental economic right.

On Affordability

The federal government has all the financial resources at its disposal to implement the Job Guarantee. But despite the program's popularity, the fight for essential public services has never been a fair one. Perhaps the most pernicious tool captains of industry have employed against policies in the public interest is the myth that federal government spending depends on the tax revenue the state can collect from them. Any struggle for economic emancipation must challenge this folktale head on, else progressive policies will be forever hostage to sound-finance ideology. To grapple with the large structural and institutional obstacles that make fighting for working people so hard, one must at a minimum confront the greatest ideological tool the rich and powerful have at their disposal: the myth that *they* pay for everything.

None of this is "easy," but there is no use pretending that the obstacles are insurmountable. Most arguments against the Job Guarantee have in the past been raised in opposition to other essential public policies. That is the nature of the politics of fear. There are no compelling moral or economic reasons to continue business as usual. It is no surprise that government employment policies are very popular, and so is the Job Guarantee, as we will see in the next and final chapter. The question is what should we fear more – a world in which a living-wage job is secured for all, or a world where mass unemployment remains the norm?

6

The Job Guarantee, the Green New Deal, and Beyond

When the Job Guarantee reentered the political discourse in the US in 2018, a number of surveys tried to gauge its popularity. A Hill-HarrisX poll from October 2019 found that a whopping 78 percent of voters supported the Job Guarantee,[1] including 71 percent of Republicans, 87 percent of Democrats, 81 percent of Independents, 78 percent of leaning Conservative, and 52 percent of strongly Conservative voters. Few policies have such overwhelming bipartisan support.

One polling firm (Civis Analytics), which used a deliberately partisan framing, still found that a majority of voters (52 percent) supported the program, including 58 percent of Obama-to-Trump voters, and 32 percent of Trump voters, calling it "one of the most popular issues we've ever polled."[2] Looking at the state level (Figure 5), another polling

Figure 5 Popular Support for the Job Guarantee

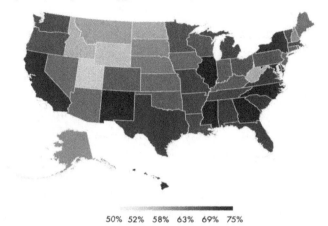

50% 52% 58% 63% 69% 75%

Source: Sean McElwee et al., "Why Democrats Should Embrace a Federal Jobs Guarantee," *The Nation*, March 20, 2018.

firm (Data for Progress) found strong support in deep Republican states as well: Mississippi (72 percent), Georgia (71 percent), Kansas (67 percent), West Virginia (62 percent), and Indiana (61 percent). Each of these states has higher-than-average unemployment and poverty rates where the Job Guarantee could have a big impact.

Once paired with the Green New Deal (GND) agenda, Data for Progress finds that overall program support increases to 55 percent.[3] When it is framed as *green*, it also becomes more popular among Trump voters by 14 percent than a Job Guarantee without the green framing.

But the public has always supported job creation and specifically programs where the government acts as an employer of last resort. A 2013 Gallup Poll reported that between 72 and 77 percent of respondents supported government employment programs and job creation *laws* that would employ the unemployed.[4]

Another study found that 68 percent of the general public believed that the government should "see to it that everyone who wants work should find a job," and 53 percent supported the idea of the government itself providing jobs to the unemployed as a last resort (Table 3).[5]

The longstanding Kinder Houston Area Study by the Kinder Institute for Urban Research has been polling since 1989 whether "the government should see to it that everyone who wants to work can find

Table 3 Support for Government Job Creation and Employer of Last Resort Policies

The government in Washington ought to see to it that everyone who wants to work can find a job	68%
The government should provide jobs for everyone who cannot find a job in private employment	53%

Source: Benjamin I. Page et al., "Democracy and the Policy Preferences of Wealthy Americans," *Perspectives on Politics*, 11, 2013: 51–73.

a job," finding consistently that over 64 percent of respondents supported the idea.[6] After the Great Financial Crisis, that number edged up to 69 percent in 2009, and by 2016, 76 percent of people believed that it was the government's responsibility to ensure that everyone who wanted a job had one. Like other polls, the Kinder survey shows that government employment policies are more popular than other income redistribution and poverty-reducing measures (Figure 6).

Figure 6 Regional Support for Government Employment Programs

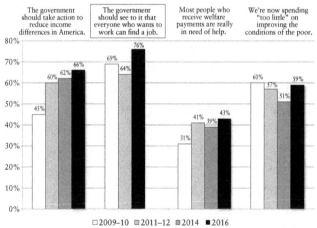

Source: Stephen L. Klineberg, "Thirty-Five Years of the Kinder Houston Area Survey: Tracking Responses to a Changing America," Houston, TX: Kinder Institute for Urban Research, 2016.

In sum, with or without a green framing, a majority of Americans support not only government employment programs, but also employer of last resort and Job Guarantee programs in particular.

Situating the Job Guarantee within the Green Agenda

This book has argued that the Job Guarantee – in purpose, design, and impact – is inherently a green proposal, addressing the two critical types of neglect and devastation in the economy – those of our natural and human resources.

While the Job Guarantee has been called the most crucial component of the Green New Deal, there is a fair amount of confusion among both critics and sympathizers about whether a net-zero emissions agenda should be muddled with policies like guaranteeing jobs, healthcare, and housing. The short answer to this question is that there are no purely technological fixes to the climate catastrophe that is barreling towards us.

Climate policy is social and economic policy. Every climate solution and the manner of its implementation will have deep economic, social, and political ramifications. To answer the question of how to tackle the climate threat is necessarily to answer the question of how to reorganize our social and economic life. The challenge before us is not just about switching techniques of production. If the inequities in the current system are not addressed, then by definition, a new technique of production would not ensure a sustainable and livable future. Would adequate housing be accessible to all if we weatherized our buildings? Would food deserts and food insecurity be wiped out if we moved from industrial to regenerative agriculture? Would gaps in public transportation be fixed if we electrified our transport systems? Would this new world provide economic security for all? Or would unemployment and poorly paid employment continue to be the norm and access to basic necessities (even if produced by green techniques) remain out of reach for many?

The living-wage Job Guarantee embeds social justice into the climate response. It recognizes that fixing the environment takes work, that many who want decent paid work cannot find it, that paid work must support traditionally undervalued activities like environmental conservation and community upkeep, and that the work experience for millions of people needs to be rehabilitated with better working conditions, essential benefits, and a sharper focus on individual and community needs. The Job Guarantee also recognizes that public service must improve the lives of those who cannot work. And while the program is not the panacea to all forms of economic insecurity or socioeconomic problems, it is the cornerstone of a modern Economic Bill of Rights – that tapestry of policies that constitute the Green New Deal agenda.

As proposed in this book, the Job Guarantee is designed around care and environmental stewardship and uses democratic and participatory processes in the creation of projects and employment opportunities. There are, however, two different ways in which the idea of "guaranteeing jobs" has been used in the contemporary climate discourse. The first, which most closely resembles the proposal in this book, aims to "guarantee a job with a family-sustaining wage, adequate family and medical leave, paid vacations, and retirement security to all people of the United States." The second focuses on "ensuring that the Green New Deal mobilization creates high-quality union jobs that pay prevailing wages, . . . and guarantees wage and benefit parity for workers affected by the transition."[7] Both of these guarantees are articulated in the Green New Deal Resolution. Some policy proposals specifically guarantee job training and priority job placement to fossil fuel workers, along with five years of their current salary or an early retirement option with pension support.[8]

How should we understand the nature of these guarantees and the way they intersect with one another?

Industrial Mobilization and the Job Guarantee

In distinguishing between the different guarantees and assurances, we need to remember that the Green New Deal too has several components: 1) it is a broad-based industrial policy; 2) it is an agenda for securing economic rights; and 3) it is a new social contract with all working people that does not leave behind those who have toiled in the fossil fuel industries for decades.

The first aspect of the Green New Deal is the wholesale transformation that is necessary to produce a rapid and robust answer to global warming. This is the all-hands-on-deck industrial strategy that has been called the "moonshot of our time" and likened to "wartime mobilization." This component requires all the technological know-how, skill, and expertise necessary to achieve the engineering feat of transforming the production system from fossil fuels to clean energy. It creates quality union jobs with prevailing wages to reverse the extraordinary hollowing-out of middle-income jobs in the labor market.

But industrial policy is not the same thing as full employment policy, though it may temporarily produce full employment during the mobilization phase of the green transformation. The second aspect of the Green New Deal thus ensures that, through a mixture of policy measures, this industrial strategy results in economic security for all. The Job Guarantee is one of those measures. It is the safety net that is especially needed by people who are most vulnerable to the ravages of climate change and most susceptible to mass layoffs in the transition process.

Finally, the Job Guarantee offers the basis for a new social contract by establishing a new labor standard, ousting unemployment as a macroeconomic stabilizer, and preventing its social and economic costs. The social contract also pays its dues, so to speak, to workers in mining and oil exploration, who have depended on the fossil fuel industry for their livelihoods and have disproportionately born the health effects of these jobs. Both low- and high-skilled fossil fuel workers would need to transition to the green economy. The skilled chemists, geologists, and engineers would join the wholesale mobilization effort perhaps more easily than the roustabouts, deckhands, and day laborers. Though, if the WWII mobilization is any indication, all manner of skills will be needed for the Green New Deal as well. For those left behind in the transition, the living-wage Job Guarantee would be a crucial safety net.

It should not be difficult to meet the promise to fossil fuel workers either. In the US, there are only about 516,000 nonsupervisory workers in the mining, quarrying, and oil and gas extraction industries (89,000 in oil and gas extraction, 148,000 in mining and quarrying, and the rest in support activities like exploration). An income safety net or early retirement can be provided for those who have toiled away on rigs and in mines, as well as generous disability support for those afflicted with black lung disease or other health problems. But for those who wish to work, the employment office would assist in finding opportunities with comparable pay in the green economy.

During the transformation, it may be hard to clearly separate mobilization jobs from Job Guarantee jobs. The proposal here is to draft separate legislation for the Job Guarantee to ensure its longevity beyond the Green New Deal. Both would require the public sector to take a leadership role in creating large-scale investment initiatives and smaller public service employment projects for those left behind. But analytically, and as a matter of legislature and institutional design, it is important to separate the two for the following reason.

Imagine that the mobilization effort has done its job, temperatures have stabilized, zero-emissions targets have been reached, and the energy grid and food production system have been transformed. What would happen next? Could we afford to honorably discharge the Job Guarantee? The answer is "no," because this transformation would not expunge the cyclical and structural variations of the economy. We failed to secure the right to work during the Roosevelt revolution, when we closed down the New Deal programs. We temporarily achieved full employment through wartime mobilization, but were unprepared to maintain full and living-wage employment for all during the peacetime postwar economy. Without an employment safety net, the goal of a useful and remunerative job for all was abandoned and the new zombie full employment concept – the NAIRU – was born. Whatever green future we produce will be neither just nor equitable if it continues to tolerate mass unemployment.

The Job Guarantee, the Green New Deal

In the 1930s, we re-envisioned the role of the state, and implemented radical policy reforms in a few short years. We created a transformative safety net, secured large-scale public investment, and passed critical labor laws. But the safer more stable economic reality was out of reach for many. Housing and school policies were segregated, women could not access the jobs and wages of their husbands, and industrial farming continued to employ immigrants, racial minorities, and the poor in the most terrible labor and living conditions. The labor standard was not secured and progress in all of these areas has been slow.

The Green New Deal is another such watershed moment. The scale of the response needed is comparable to what was required to tackle the Great Depression and a second devastating world war. The policies we design today would usher in a new economy. In the big battle to save the planet, implementing the Job Guarantee is a comparatively small but critical component. If the Green New Deal brings a broader socialization of investment in essential public goods – transportation, housing, electricity, healthcare and childcare – economic volatility would decline much the same way it did after WWII. (Prior to the New Deal of the 1930s, the US economy had experienced a depression every twenty years, and many smaller downturns in between.) The Green New Deal holds the promise of stabilizing the economy in comparable ways. However, it will not end the business cycle. While cyclical fluctuations will hardly be expunged, the fact that they are smaller would mean that the size of the Job Guarantee would also be smaller. As a permanent part of the policy landscape, it would continue to provide an employment safety net and a macroeconomic stabilization mechanism, even as we transition to a cleaner, more stable and more just economy.

Conclusion: The Missing Global Employment Policy

By focusing on the US case, we have run the risk of suggesting that the Job Guarantee is a policy option accessible only to economic hegemons. This is not the case, not least because some of the largest job creation programs, and the only introduction of a legal right to employment, have been implemented in developing countries (South Africa, Argentina, India). Economic hegemons can of course lead the way, but a global pledge to tackle unemployment once and for all would not be unprecedented. The world came to a similar conclusion after WWII when it drafted the International Trade Organization (ITO) charter.[9] Explicit in the first two chapters was a clear global mandate to ensure that each nation implemented policies for *attaining and maintaining full employment* over the long run as a precondition for free trade. When the ITO was not ratified and the WTO succeeded it, the "full employment" mandate was dropped from the agenda. Today, many nations rely on export-led growth for job creation and engage in race-to-the-bottom labor practices to win what is essentially an unwinnable job-creation war. Unemployment and precarious employment are global phenomena.

Today the global community is engaged in a new conversation, not about how to integrate peacefully through trade, but about how to address the planetary climate emergency. Global institutions and international accords require a commitment to full and decent employment the same way global trade once required it but failed to achieve it. The 2015 Paris Agreement was an important first step, highlighting that climate justice rests on "human rights, . . . the imperatives of a just transition of the workforce, and the creation of decent work and quality jobs in accordance with nationally defined development priorities."[10]

The Job Guarantee, the Green New Deal

While the Job Guarantee proposal presented here has been pitched as a nation-specific policy, it could form the basis of a Global Marshall Plan that tackles the twin threats of environmental and economic insecurity. No workfare, no "bullshit jobs," no compulsory work, no digging holes. A global Green New Deal with a green Job Guarantee.

Notes

Introduction

1 Robinson Meyer, "The Democratic Party Wants to Make Climate Policy Exciting," *The Atlantic*, December 5, 2018.
2 William S. Vickrey, *Full Employment and Price Stability: The Macroeconomic Vision of William S. Vickrey*, edited by Mathew Forstater and Pavlina R. Tcherneva, Edward Elgar, 2004.

Chapter 1

1 The broader measure would include people who want to work but are not counted because they did not look for work in the survey week, or those who work part-time because they cannot find full-time work. For details see, e.g., Flavia Dantas and L. Randall Wray, "Full Employment: Are We There Yet?," Levy Economics Institute, Public Policy Brief No. 142, 2017.
2 Pavlina R. Tcherneva, "Reorienting Fiscal Policy: A Bottom-up Approach," *Journal of Post Keynesian Economics*, 37(1), 2014: 43–66.
3 T. Piketty and E. Saez, "Income Inequality in the United

States, 1913–1998," *Quarterly Journal of Economics*, 118(1), 2019 [2003]: 1–39.

4 Nina McCollum, "What I've Learned About Unemployment and Being Poor After Applying for 215 Jobs," *HuffPost*, July 26, 2019.

5 Alexia Fernández Campbell, "A Loophole in Federal Law Allows Companies to Pay Disabled Workers $1 an Hour," *Vox*, May 3, 2018.

6 Liz Goodwin, "Job Listings Say the Unemployed Need Not Apply," *Yahoo News*, July 26, 2011.

7 "A Profile of the Working Poor, 2017: BLS Reports," US Bureau of Labor Statistics, United States Department of Labor, April 2019.

Chapter 2

1 Remarks made at the American Economic Association conference, January 2019, emphasis added.

2 "Why Do Interest Rates Matter?," Board of Governors of the Federal Reserve System, September 9, 2016.

3 "Federal Reserve Chair Jerome Powell Testimony on the State of the Economy", House Financial Services Committee, July 10, 2019, www.c-span.org/video/?46 2331-1/fed-chair-warns-weakening-economic-growth-pled ges-serve-full-year-term.

4 "How Does Monetary Policy Influence Inflation and Employment?," Board of Governors of the Federal Reserve System, December 16, 2015.

5 Matthew C. Klein, "Debunking the NAIRU Myth," *Financial Times*, January 19, 2017.

6 Olivier Blanchard, "Should We Reject the Natural Rate Hypothesis?," *Journal of Economic Perspectives*, 32(1), 2018: 97–120.

7 Sam Fleming, "Fed Has No Reliable Theory of Inflation, Says Tarullo," *Financial Times*, October 4, 2017.

8 Emanuel A. Goldenweiser et al., "Jobs, Production and

Living Standards," *Board of Governors of the Federal Reserve System (US) Postwar Economic Studies*, August 1945, emphasis added.

9 Ibid.

10 Giuliano Bonoli, "Employers' Attitudes towards Long-Term Unemployed People and the Role of Activation in Switzerland," *International Journal of Social Welfare*, 23(4), 2014: 421–30.

11 Liz Goodwin, "Job Listings Say the Unemployed Need Not Apply," *Yahoo News*, July 26, 2011.

12 Stefan Eriksson and Dan-Olof Rooth, "Do Employers Use Unemployment as a Sorting Criterion When Hiring? Evidence from a Field Experiment," *American Economic Review*, 104(3), 2014: 1014–39.

13 Alicia S. Modestino et al., "Upskilling: Do Employers Demand Greater Skill When Workers Are Plentiful?," *Review of Economics and Statistics* (forthcoming).

14 Katherine Weisshaar, "From Opt Out to Blocked Out: The Challenges for Labor Market Re-Entry after Family-Related Employment Lapses," *American Sociological Review*, 83(1), 2018: 34–60.

15 Devah Pager, *Marked: Race, Crime, and Finding Work in an Era of Mass Incarceration*, University of Chicago Press, 2009.

16 Barbara Goldberg, "Disabled Workers Chase 'Dream Jobs' in Tight US Labor Market," *Reuters*, August 30, 2019.

17 One for the US, created by FlowingData, is available here: www.youtube.com/watch?v=shqJR_0WdrI.

18 Anne Case and Angus Deaton, "Rising Morbidity and Mortality in Midlife among White Non-Hispanic Americans in the 21st Century," *Proceedings of the National Academy of Sciences*, 112(49), 2015: 15078–83.

19 Carlos Nordt et al., "Modelling Suicide and Unemployment: A Longitudinal Analysis Covering 63 Countries, 2000–11," *The Lancet Psychiatry*, 2(3), 2015: 239–45.

20 Christian Breuer and Horst Rottmann, "Do Labor Market

Institutions Influence Suicide Mortality? An International Panel Data Analysis," CESifo Working Paper Series No. 4875, Munich: Center for Economic Studies and Ifo Institute, 2014.

21 D. Stuckler and S. Basu, *The Body Economic: Why Austerity Kills*, Basic Books, 2013.

22 Kenneth A. Couch et al., "Economic and Health Implications of Long-Term Unemployment: Earnings, Disability Benefits, and Mortality," *Research in Labor Economics*, 38, 2013: 259–305.

23 Katharine G. Abraham et al., "The Consequences of Long-Term Unemployment: Evidence from Linked Survey and Administrative Data," NBER Working Paper No. 22665, September 2016.

24 Margaret W. Linn et al., "Effects of Unemployment on Mental and Physical Health," *American Journal of Public Health*, 75(5), 1985: 502–6.

25 Karsten I. Paul and Klaus Moser, "Unemployment Impairs Mental Health: Meta-Analyses," *Journal of Vocational Behavior*, 74(3), 2009: 264–82.

26 Alan B. Krueger, "Where Have All the Workers Gone? An Inquiry into the Decline of the US Labor Force Participation Rate," *Brookings Papers on Economic Activity*, September 2, 2017: 1–87.

27 Lars Kunze and Nicolai Suppa, "Bowling Alone or Bowling at All? The Effect of Unemployment on Social Participation," Ruhr Economic Paper No. 510, October 2014.

28 Rainer Winkelmann and Liliana Winkelmann, "Unemployment: Where Does it Hurt?," Center for Economic and Policy Research, CEPR Discussion Paper No. 1093, 1995.

29 Melisa Bubonya et al., "A Family Affair: Job Loss and the Mental Health of Spouses and Adolescents," IZA Discussion Paper No. 8588, December 3, 2014; Joanna Venator and Richard Reeve, "Parental Unemployment

Hurts Kid's Futures and Social Mobility," The Brookings Institution, Social Mobility Memos, 2013.

30 Steven Raphael and Rudolf Winter-Ebmer, "Identifying the Effect of Unemployment on Crime," *Journal of Law and Economics*, 44(1), 2001: 259–83.

31 Richard Freeman, "Crime and the Employment of Disadvantaged Youths," in *Urban Labor Markets and Job Opportunity*, edited by George Peterson and Wayne Vroman, Urban Institute Press, 1992; Armin Falk and Josef Zweimuller, "Unemployment and Right-Wing Extremist Crime," Centre for Economic Policy Research, CEPR Discussion Paper No. 4997, 2005.

32 According to the International Youth Foundation, if we account for measurement limitations, youth unemployment may be six to seven times higher than the ILO estimates.

33 Mark T. Berg and Beth M. Huebner, "Reentry and the Ties that Bind: An Examination of Social Ties, Employment, and Recidivism," *Justice Quarterly*, 28(2), 2011: 382–410.

34 James K. Galbraith, "Inequality, Unemployment and Growth: New Measures for Old Controversies," *The Journal of Economic Inequality*, 7(2), 2009: 189–206.

35 William Darity, "Who Loses from Unemployment," *Journal of Economic Issues*, 33(2), 1999: 491–6.

36 James K. Galbraith, *Created Unequal: The Crisis in American Pay*, Free Press, 1998.

37 William Mitchell, "The Costs of Unemployment – Again," 2012, http://bilbo.economicoutlook.net/blog/?p=17740; methodology in Martin J. Watts and William F. Mitchell, "The Costs of Unemployment in Australia," *The Economic and Labour Relations Review*, 11(2), 2000: 180–97.

Chapter 3

1 Ganesh Sitaraman and Anne Alstott, *The Public Option: How to Expand Freedom, Increase Opportunity, and Promote Equality*, Harvard University Press, 2019.

2   William F. Mitchell, "The Buffer Stock Employment Model and the NAIRU: The Path to Full Employment," *Journal of Economic Issues*, 32(2), 1998: 547–55.

3   The US government maintained grain buffer stock programs, including for wheat and corn, well into the late 1970s.

4   The argument follows Robert E. Prasch, "How is Labor Distinct from Broccoli? Some Unique Characteristics of Labor and their Importance for Economic Analysis and Policy," in *The Institutionalist Tradition in Labor Economics*, edited by Dell P. Champlin and Janet T. Knoedler, M.E. Sharpe, 2004.

5   Isobel Asher Hamilton, "Amazon is Raising Its Minimum Wage to \$15 Following Pressure from Bernie Sanders," *Business Insider*, October 2, 2018.

6   Paul K. Sonn and Yannet Lathrop, "Raise Wages, Kill Jobs? Seven Decades of Historical Data Find No Correlation Between Minimum Wage Increases and Employment Levels," National Employment Law Project, May 5, 2016.

7   Alanna Petroff, "German Workers Win Right to 28-Hour Week," *CNN Business*, February 7, 2018.

8   Kevin Whitman et al., "Who Never Receives Social Security Benefits?," *Social Security Bulletin*, 71(2), 2011, at https://www.ssa.gov/policy/docs/ssb/v71n2/v71n2p17.html.

9   Tressie McMillan Cottom, "Raising the Floor, Not Just the Ceiling," *Slate Magazine*, January 23, 2014.

Chapter 4

1   L. Randall Wray, *Modern Money Theory: A Primer on Macroeconomics for Sovereign Monetary Systems*, Palgrave Macmillan, 2012.

2   Beardsley Ruml, "Taxes for Revenue are Obsolete," *American Affairs*, 8(1), 1946: 35–9.

3   Ben S. Bernanke, Interview with CBS program *60 Minutes*, March 15, 2009.

4 "Estimated Impact of the American Recovery and Reinvestment Act on Employment and Economic Output in 2014," Congressional Budget Office, 2015, https://www.cbo.gov/publication/49958.

5 "Archive of Monthly Unemployment Data," National Jobs for All Coalition, https://njfac.org/index.php/jobs-and-job-security/405–2.

6 Pavlina R. Tcherneva, "Obama's Job Creation Promise," Policy Note 2009/1, Annandale-on- Hudson, NY: Levy Economics Institute of Bard College, 2009.

7 Jason Wiens, "Entrepreneurship's Role in Economic Development," *Entrepreneurship Policy Digest*, June 11, 2014.

8 Living Wage Calculator, MIT, https://livingwage.mit.edu.

9 Abigail Hess, "California is Paying Inmates $1 an Hour to Fight Wildfires," *CNBC*, November 12, 2018.

10 L. Randall Wray et al., "Public Service Employment: A Path to Full Employment," Levy Institute Research Project Report, Annandale-on-Hudson, NY: Levy Economics Institute of Bard College, 2018.

Chapter 5

1 See, for example, Philip Harvey, *Securing the Right to Employment: Social Welfare Policy and the Unemployed in the United States*, Princeton University Press, 1989. See also, William Darity and Darrick Hamilton, "Full Employment and the Job Guarantee: An All-American Idea," in *Full Employment and Social Justice*, edited by Michael Murray and Matthew Forstater, Palgrave Macmillan, 2017, pp. 195–204.

2 "H.R. 1000 – 115th Congress: Jobs for All Act," 2017, https://www.congress.gov/bill/115th-congress/house-bill/1000.

3 Sandra Opdycke, *The WPA: Creating Jobs and Hope in the Great Depression*, Routledge, 2016.

4 John C. Paige, *The Civilian Conservation Corps and the National Park Service: 1933–1942. An Administrative History*, US Government Publishing Office, 1985.

5 Nick Taylor, *American-Made: The Enduring Legacy of the WPA: When FDR Put the Nation to Work*, Bantam Books, 2009.

6 Pavlina R. Tcherneva, "Beyond Full Employment: What Argentina's *Plan Jefes* Can Teach Us about the Employer of Last Resort," in *Employment Guarantee Schemes*, edited by Michael Murray and Matthew Forstater, Palgrave Macmillan, 2013.

7 Neelakshi Mann and Varad Pande, *Mgnrega Sameeksha: An Anthology of Research Studies on the Mahatma Gandhi National Rural Employment Guarantee Act, 2005, 2006–2012*, Orient Blackswan, 2012.

8 Tanweer Ali, "The UK Future Jobs Fund: The Labour Party's Adoption of the Job Guarantee," Post-Keynesian Economics Study Group, Working Paper 1106, September 1, 2013.

9 "Albuquerque Mayor: Here's a Crazy Idea, Let's Give Homeless People Jobs," *PBS NewsHour*, November 26, 2015.

10 "Ready4Work, a Prisoner Reentry Initiative," City of Jacksonville, Office of the Mayor, https://www.coj.net/mayor/docs/the-jacksonville-journey/ready4work-whitepaper1107-(2).aspx.

11 James K. Galbraith, "We Work," *The Baffler*, May 2, 2018.

12 Noah Smith, "A Federal Job Guarantee is Asking for Trouble," *Bloomberg*, March 11, 2019.

13 Philip Harvey, *Securing the Right to Employment: Social Welfare Policy and the Unemployed in the United States*, Princeton University Press, 1989.

14 Ibid.

15 David Cooper, "Raising the Federal Minimum Wage

to $15 by 2024 Would Lift Pay for Nearly 40 Million Workers," Economic Policy Institute, February 2019.

16 Katie Allen, "Technology Has Created More Jobs Than It Has Destroyed Says 140 Years of Data," *The Guardian*, August 18, 2015.

17 "H.Res.109 – 116th Congress: Recognizing the Duty of the Federal Government to Create a Green New Deal," 2019, https://www.congress.gov/116/bills/hres109/BILLS-116hres109ih.pdf.

18 "Jobs for All: A Pledge," https://jobguaranteenow.org.

19 Michael Kalecki, "Political Aspects of Full Employment," *Political Quarterly*, 14(4), 1943: 322–30.

Chapter 6

1 "Majority of Voters Support a Federal Jobs Guarantee Program," *The Hill*, October 30, 2019.

2 Sean McElwee et al., "Why Democrats Should Embrace a Federal Jobs Guarantee," *The Nation*, March 20, 2018.

3 Kate Aronoff, "All of a Sudden, Adding 'Green' to a Policy Idea Makes It More Popular," *The Intercept*, September 21, 2018.

4 Jeffrey M. Jones, "Americans Widely Back Government Job Creation Proposals," *Gallup*, March 14, 2013.

5 Benjamin I. Page et al., "Democracy and the Policy Preferences of Wealthy Americans," *Perspectives on Politics*, 11, 2013: 51–73.

6 Stephen L. Klineberg, "Thirty-Five Years of the Kinder Houston Area Survey: Tracking Responses to a Changing America," Houston, TX: Kinder Institute for Urban Research, 2016.

7 "H.Res.109 – 116th Congress: Recognizing the Duty of the Federal Government to Create a Green New Deal," 2019, https://www.congress.gov/116/bills/hres109/BILLS-116hres109ih.pdf.

8 "The Green New Deal," *Bernie Sanders Official Campaign*

Website, https://berniesanders.com/en/issues/green-new-deal.

9 Pavlina R. Tcherneva, "A Global Marshall Plan for Joblessness?," *Institute for New Economic Thinking*, May 11, 2016.

10 United Nations, Paris Agreement, United Nations Treaty Collection, 2015, https://unfccc.int/sites/default/files/english_paris_agreement.pdf.

Index

139

Index

Index

Index

Index

Index

Index

Index

Index